#startupeverywhere

Startup Guide London

Editor: Jenna van Uden
Writers: Lee Bell and Senay Boztas
Copyeditor: Laurence Currie-Clark
Proofreader: Josh Raisher

Art direction, design & layout by
Design Studio Maurice Redmond - Berlin
www.dsmr.berlin

Illustrations by sanjini.com

London Team
Project Director: Jeanette Carlsson
Project Manager: Kate Nield
Photographer: Anders Birger
Researcher: Ingibjörg Ferrer

Additional photography by
Alex Asensi, Daniela Carducci,
Celia Topping, Camilo Gutierrez,
and unsplash.com

Printed in Berlin, Germany by
Medialis-Offsetdruck GmbH
Heidelberger Str. 65, 12435 Berlin

Published by Startup Everywhere
Vestergade 82, 3 TV. Aarhus, Denmark
info@startupeverywhere.com

Visit: startupeverywhere.com

ISBN 978-87-93412-07-1

STARTUP GUIDE
LONDON

STARTUP GUIDE LONDON

In partnership with **newmedia2.0**

Proudly supported by

startup.focus.

Future Cities

Department for
International Trade

Sadiq Khan
/ Mayor of London

London is – as it always has been – where the world comes to do business. We are home to some of the world's great institutions of banking, insurance and consulting. A city of innovation, of ideas and of exciting new talent, our future is bright as a world leader in digital technology.

We are attracting record levels of inward investment from companies who see the city as the gateway to Europe. And we are the leading European center for technology and life sciences, with our world-leading universities attracting thousands of international students. This is one of the most desirable cities to live and work in, and is the most open, welcoming and cosmopolitan city in Europe. More than 300 languages are spoken here and more than a third of our residents were born overseas. We remain the world's most popular city as a tourist destination, and welcomed a record 18.6 million international visitors in 2015.

I'm passionate about supporting digital technology and innovation, and I am committed to doing everything that I can to share the message that London is open to the world's brightest minds and best ideas. We will do everything possible to help our tech sector to flourish, and I hope to see many more great tech companies and entrepreneurs coming to London to start and grow their businesses.

Sadiq Khan

London, England

[Key Features]

- A huge number of startups: over **275,000** companies which employ nearly **1.5 m** people. Since 2005, these companies have raised **€8.3 billion.**

- Low administrative barriers to new company formation.

- A strong financial sector that favors fintech and crowdfunding startups.

- Home of several world-leading universities such as Imperial, UCL, Kings and London School of Economics.

- More 'unicorns' (billion-dollar startups) than any other European city, which helps provide visible role models and experienced mentors.

- Extremely high cost of living: very high housing and office rental costs.

- High cost of talent (higher than elsewhere) – those with digital skills are in particularly high demand.

Notable startups:

Scaleups:
- food ordering and delivery platform Deliveroo (raised **€87.5 m**)
- online e-commerce platform Made.com (raised **€71 m**)
- advertising software company AppNexus (raised **€253.5 m**)
- loans company Borro (raised **€150.8 m**).

Unicorns:
- media engagement app Shazam (raised **€114 m**)
- peer-to-peer money transfer service Transferwise (raised **€79.5 m**)
- online payday lender Wonga (raised **€127.8 m**)
- global community of fashion boutiques FarFetch (raised **€171 m**).

Founders would consider starting up in London for the following top reasons:

[Ecosystem]

14.4%

[Access to Capital]

14.8%

[Access to Talent]

14.4%

[Burn Rate]

14.3%

[Rank]

City Ranking

European founders had up to 5 votes from a list of 30 cities

1. Berlin
2. **London**
3. Amsterdam
4. Barcelona
5. Lisbon

6. Dublin
7. Stockholm
8. Munich
9. Copenhagen
10. Vienna

STARTUP GUIDE LONDON

Sources: European Digital Index 2016, Startup Heatmap Europe 2016

Local Community Partner

newmedia2.0

Helping startups and scale-ups grow, and corporates adopt more entrepreneurial approaches to innovation, is what we love to do. The UK, led by London, has one of the most diverse startup ecosystems in the world, which – despite #Brexit – continues to receive more investment than any other European city.

As leading independent advisors playing a key role in the London startup sector, newmedia2.0 offers startups (and other companies) help to shape their propositions, business and marketing strategies, find investors and partners, build teams and skills, go to market, launch and growth plans, and connect with our substantial network. We have worked with a high number of UK and international startups, who come to London to set up and grow their businesses, helped investors and corporates find startups, and led design hackathons and innovation programs (e.g., smart city/urban innovation), offering startups opportunities to meet established firms and the public sector to innovate and create new partnerships. We also offer a London Digital Learning program, lecture on innovation and entrepreneurship at leading UK universities, and have advised the UK Government and Connecting Tech City steering group.

We work closely with London's leading technology network Tech London Advocates, Tech City, Greater London Authority (GLA), London and Partners, Future Cities Catapult, Here East and many of London's other key private and public sector organizations working to support London's startup sector. Finally, we have founded and chaired Tech Nordic Advocates, Northern Europe's largest network of tech leaders from entrepreneurs to startups, scale-ups, mentors, experts, investors and established tech company leaders – the first non-UK off-shoot of Tech London Advocates and Global Tech Advocates (see Russ Shaw 'Interviews') – offering London startups and scale-ups an international network and platform for growth into other global startup and tech hubs.

newmedia2.0 are committed to supporting London startups, and proud to have been selected to produce this Guide – a fitting tribute to London as Europe's leading startup hub. We hope with Startup Guide London, we can help more entrepreneurs navigate the London startup landscape, and facilitate their journeys to becoming successful businesses, built and grown in London.

Jeanette Carlsson
CEO, newmedia2.0

STARTUP GUIDE LONDON

spaces

experts

interviews

London Essentials

London is home to more companies than any other city in Europe, and according to the Inc. 5000 Europe List 2016 is the fastest city for high growth businesses on the continent.

This growth is reflected across the whole city, with coworking spaces and startup accelerators popping up in all corners of the capital. Venture capital funding has improved too. Thanks to the growing number of high-profile accelerator programs and a government mission to prioritize the growing fintech sector, there are fewer barriers to securing funding in London. Heralded as Europe's biggest metropolitan melting pot of language, religion and culture, London is growing and growing fast.

Before You Come

There are a few things you should get out of the way before landing in London. Getting a National Insurance number is imperative to live and work in the UK. It is a unique personal account number used to ensure that the National Insurance contributions and tax you pay are properly recorded on your account. The process of getting a National Insurance number can take up to several weeks, so plan ahead and book an appointment on the phone before arriving. The kind of visa you can apply for depends on your own country's agreement with the UK and the type of business you'll be setting up. Check with your embassy and relevant government institutions (**gov.uk/check-uk-visa**). Ensure you have health insurance coverage while you get set up and that you have paperwork to prove who you are, such as a passport or other documents. You will need to show landlords and leasing agents your identity papers too so they can check that you have leave to stay in the UK. It is ideal to have enough saved to cover up to three months' rent for a security deposit. House hunting in London can be stressful, so arrange for accommodation while you get on your feet.

Cost of Living

Asking locals for recommendations on where to eat and drink is always a good idea. Generally, a basic lunchtime menu in the business district will set you back £10. According to **expatistan.com**, utilities for one month in an 85 m² flat will cost around £204 for two people, and the hourly rate for cleaning help starts at £11. The Family and Childcare Trust Survey for 2016 reports that fifty hours childcare a week for a child under two in London in a nursery is £302.17, and with a childminder is £286.48. A dinner for two in a neighborhood pub will cost around £35, while a dinner for two at an Italian restaurant, including appetizers, main course, wine and dessert, will be around £68. Restaurants located next to big landmarks may be more costly.

Cultural Differences

It's no exaggeration to say that London is one of the most multicultural cities in the world. You could eat a different meal out every night and still taste something new. The joy with London is that there's never a dull moment. This can get a bit hectic of course, which is why there are so many beautiful parks and pubs to relax in – but with so many famous museums and galleries, world-class theater and nightlife, and countless hidden gems to seek out, it's impossible to just stay indoors. With the right attitude and spirit of adventure, you will see and do things that you won't see anywhere else. So explore, enjoy and experience it for yourself.

Renting an Apartment

Finding a place to stay in London can be hard, even for existing residents. Rooms for rent are snapped up just as quickly as they become available. The best places to find a room on late notice are sites such as Kangaroom. If you want to do it the more conventional way, however, and go through an estate agent, Zoopla, Right Move and OpenRent are the most popular options, but are better suited to those looking for a whole apartment to rent. As in all cities, it is important to carry out checks on private landlords. The median price of renting a one bed-room flat or studio generally ranges from £700 to £2,000, depending on the size and location. Staying with friends at the beginning can give you a base for checking out potential places. You will need to be on your toes if you want to secure the room you want.

See **Flats and Rentals** page 226

Finding a Coworking Space

London is brimming with shared places to work, and it's a good idea to spend a day cycling, bussing or tubing around the city to see which one best caters to your needs. Some have larger offices on offer, such as Here East, and some you will need to apply to in advance due to high demand – for example, Rainmaking Loft, which has branches spread across the city. Others are smaller, and working in a kooky office – maybe next to a mini golf course, like at Runway East – might be just the thing to inspire you. Some places offer whole offices that you can fit out yourself (for example, TechSpace), while others have spacious areas where entrepreneurs can join easily and cheaply (like TMRW). If you're in need of something more suave, there will be something for you at Interchange, designed by DRS under Tom Dixon. For a map of coworking spaces in London go to **growthhub.london**. The web page is funded by the Mayor of London, and provides free advice on premises as well as business support.

See **Spaces** page 66

Insurance

Thanks to the NHS, the UK has one of the best national health systems in the world, free at the point of use for all its citizens. As long as Britain is part of the EU, citizens of member nations can access the NHS for free as part of a reciprocal EU healthcare agreement via their European Health Insurance Card (EHIC). An EHIC can be obtained from your home EU nation. If you are coming to the UK from outside the EU for more than six months, you will be required to pay a health surcharge at the time of your visa application. This will give you access to the NHS until the time of your visa renewal, when the health surcharge will apply again. If leave to remain is granted you can then access the NHS just like any other citizen. Health insurance is an optional extra which you might want to arrange for additional peace of mind. Some employers in the UK also offer health insurance as part of their additional benefits to employees. For more information on accessing the NHS as a visitor or immigrant to the UK, please visit **nhs.uk**.

See **Insurance Companies** page 227

Visas and Work Permits

If you're looking to start a business in London and you're from outside the European Economic Area (EEA) and Switzerland, you could apply for a Tier 1 (Entrepreneur) visa. To apply, you must be able to prove you have access to at least £50,000 in investment funds. The earliest you can apply is three months before you travel, and you should get a decision on your visa within three weeks. It is worth noting that this will cost £1,204 if you apply online or by post, and £963 if you apply in person outside the UK (**gov.uk/tier-1-entrepreneur/overview**). You can work in the UK for a maximum of three years and four months with this visa. Other options could be to study first in higher education and get permission to work, then look at the Graduate Entrepreneur route to start up your business. While the UK remains a member of the EU, EU and EEA nationals have permission to live and work in the UK.

See **Important Government Offices** page 226

Starting a Company

Registering a business in the UK is quite straightforward, particularly compared to other European countries. However, you may wish to seek advice as to the best way to register your company to suit your activities. Most businesses can be registered as a sole trader, limited company or 'ordinary' partnership. It's simpler to set up as a sole trader, but you're personally responsible for your business' debts. You also have some accounting responsibilities. If you form a limited company, its finances are separate from your personal finances, but there are more reporting and management responsibilities. An 'ordinary' partnership is the simplest way for two or more people to run a business together as you share responsibility for your business' debts and each have accounting responsibilities as well. If you take on your own employees, agency workers or freelancers, you have some other responsibilities, such as running payroll, paying for their National Insurance and providing workplace pensions. Getting into a good coworking space, incubator or accelerator to begin with, where costs will be significantly less and you'll get help with getting up and running, might be a good idea. Visit **gov.uk** for more information on setting up a business.

See **Programs** page 50

Opening a Bank Account

To set up a bank account in the UK you'll need your National Insurance number, so make sure you sort that out first. Most banks require that you already have a job and address in the UK before opening an account, so give your chosen banks a call to be clear on their requirements before setting those wheels in motion. Popular bank chains in the UK include Barclays, Halifax, HSBC, Lloyds Bank, NatWest, Royal Bank of Scotland and TSB. They each have varying levels of interest offerings depending on current promotions, so it is worth shopping around.

See **Banks** page 225

Taxes

Tax contributions in the UK differ depending on how the business is organized (e.g., whether it is sole trader or partnership). With so many complicated tax rules currently in place, it can be difficult to know exactly which ones apply to you, so seek advice from HMRC (Her Majesty's Revenue and Customs) if you're unsure. There are a few common taxes you will have to pay as a small business owner. The main ones are: income tax, which you pay on your business' profit once it goes over the personal allowance of £11,000; corporation tax, which is currently 20 percent for all companies; and VAT, which you'll have to register for if you make a turnover of more than £83,000 a year. Other income sources such as income from savings, investments and property would count towards the personal allowances. Because keeping on top of taxes can be difficult on your own, most businesses, large and small, and even freelancers, will hire accountants to keep bookkeeping in order – this is highly recommended if you seek accounting advice. Visit **gov.uk** for more information on registering your business and business tax.

See **Accountants** page 225

Telephone Contracts

Mobile phone signal varies throughout the UK. If you're planning on traveling in and out of London a lot, look for a network that has no additional roaming fees in foreign destinations. Broadband contracts work in the same way; shop around and call to see if you can get a good deal. While it can be tempting to just pick the cheapest deal you can find, going over your limit could land you with hefty bills for calls or data not covered by your plan. If you're unsure who to go with, opt for a pay as you go SIM-only deal for your existing phone to start with, and get a feel for the network before committing to a contract, which will generally last for 24 months. Alternatively, temporary-use SIM cards are available from most high street technology retailers.

Getting Around

London's world-famous public transport system means you won't need a car to get around. It's one of the largest networks in the world and services are fully integrated, so it's easy to switch between them to get around. But it is more expensive than in some other places. As a result, the new mayor has frozen TfL fares until 2020 and introduced a new 'Hopper' ticket so that you can change buses without having to pay twice. You can now use a contactless bank card on most services, which will save time and money; you won't need to stop to top-up an Oyster card or buy a ticket.

More and more Londoners are choosing to cycle to get around. It's fast, healthy and becoming safer as new protected cycle lanes are built across town. In central London, you can also hire a bike from as little as £2 from one of the 700 docking stations.

Learning the Language

If you need to brush up on your English skills, check out the London School of English, a well-established institute with a range of courses depending on your needs aimed at those with a basic understanding looking to polish their skills. London universities offer a number of English language programs suitable for all levels, including the University of London, King's College London and UCL.

See **Language Schools** page 227

Meeting People

Shared office spaces – especially those with accommodation attached – are an obvious way to start building a network in London. All of the main accelerators and incubators offering offices and development programs for startups run meetings, sessions and talks, so go along to these. Network, network and network – London is a great place for making new acquaintances.

See **Startup Events** page 227

ups

LEMONADE

[Name]
Giraffe360

[Elevator Pitch]
"Giraffe360 technology enables the real estate industry to elevate property viewing into a virtual reality experience using simple 360 virtual tour camera technology."

[The Story]
Giraffe360 has roots in Latvia, where CEO Mikus Opelts and a group of friends met in college in 2010. Lacking resources but brimming with ideas and passion, the young students built a virtual tour service for European companies, producing high-end virtual tours for big brands like Hilton and Colliers to dramatically increase remote property presentations. But while Mikus and his team managed to increase efficiency for businesses and provide much better service for clients, scaling the service and making a difference in the market were harder than they first thought.

In a bid to make a solution that wasn't too expensive for mass use, Mikus and his brother Madars Opelts, Giraffe360 CTO and cofounder, made a ten-minute decision to move to London due to its good reputation for startup culture. The duo drew up some rough plans for what they believed the 'world's best virtual tour technology' should look like, with a price point under property photography costs. With these two things set, the brothers spent the next year building what is now Giraffe360, integrating hardware, software and VR with web and mobile apps. Giraffe360 consists of an easy-to-use camera that generates HDR images, which are automatically stitched together in the Giraffe360 software to create a high-quality virtual tour experience that anyone can create and view, making property tours possible from anywhere in the world.

[Funding History]

Bootstrap

[Milestones]
- Kicking off the virtual tour service business in 2010 with no money in the bank
- Turning over 500K in 2015
- Building the Giraffe360 technology startup
- Finishing the first fully working prototype in June 2016

[Links]   Website: **giraffe360.com** Facebook: **giraffevisual** Twitter: **@Giraffe360** Instagram: **Giraffe360**

[Name]
The Memo

[Elevator Pitch]
"The Memo is an online publication covering modern business and lifestyle. Our mission is to make the future more human."

[The Story]
The Memo was conceived in 2014 by Alex Wood, a former technology journalist with ten years experience covering London startups at the BBC, Bloomberg and Tech City News. The idea for The Memo materialized from Alex's observation of the growing nature of technology and the increasing impact it was having on people's personal and professional lives.

'I felt there was a gap in the market for something that explained what changes in technology meant to people outside of the industry,' says Alex. 'It's not like those outside the tech profession can escape it, so I thought we needed a publication that speaks about the impact of technology in a language people want to hear.'

The voice of The Memo was developed from Alex's increasing appearances on TV and radio. With a broadcast background, he found his forte was in seeing through complicated ideas and explaining them in a concise and relatable way, all of which tied in well with the tone he wanted to create for his publication. And so The Memo was born, following the same purpose: 'To make the future more human.' The Memo attracted industry titan PWC as a launch sponsor, buying into what Alex was trying to create and supporting him from day one.

[Funding History]

Angel Investment   Seed Funding

[Milestones]
- Winning the first client, PWC, as a launch sponsor
- Winning four industry awards, including The Drum's Online Media Awards' Best Site for Journalism
- Being contacted for Brexit coverage by the likes of Radio 4 and Sky News
- Hitting highest ever traffic figures in October 2016; making a profit just 18 months after starting up

[Links]   Website: **thememo.com** Facebook: **thememotech** Twitter: **@theMemo** Instagram: **thememohq**

[Name] # Linden Staub

[Elevator Pitch] *"We are a unique newcomer to the modelling industry, a 100 percent mother agency that represents and books talent in the UK. Run by females for females, we work in the models' interests, giving a voice to the exploited faces."*

[The Story] Born out of frustration with politics in the modelling world, Linden Staub was created by Esther Kinnear-Derungs and Tara Davies, a pair that had worked together at a modelling agency for a combined ten years. They loved their jobs, but were feeling increasingly disillusioned with how women were treated in the industry: Models being placed in the wrong agencies, girls being pulled and people not working for the models and their careers. One night, over a glass of wine, Esther and Tara toyed with the idea of creating their own 100 percent mother agency, a business that books and represents. Knowing that London was the perfect city for this kind of agency because of its dynamic market, the pair set the wheels in motion. They discussed the idea in more detail for two weeks, talked it over with their families and set up the logistics.

'There was no real "lightbulb moment",' says Tara. 'More a realization that grew in time and confidence in our minds.' The process of getting Linden Staub off the ground was relatively easy for the duo, as they both knew the industry inside out. 'The only thing that took time was logistics, such as finding an office and getting contracts written up,' added Tara. 'The rest felt like it took two seconds.' The pair formed the company in December 2015, and launched officially in March.

[Funding History]

Venture Capital

[Milestones]
- Developing a unique idea for an agency in a very saturated market
- Setting up an amazing network of people to work with
- First British New Face launching on a Gucci Resort show exclusive
- Losing a new face to competition and learning to tighten the development stages contractually

[Links] Website: **lindenstaub.com** Facebook: **LindenStaub** Twitter: **@LindenStaub** Instagram: **lindenstaub**

[Name] # Seenit

[Elevator Pitch] *"We're changing the way companies think about producing video by collaborating with employees, customers and experts to capture video anytime, anywhere in the world. Through our technology we focus on this content to produce the most honest and real stories."*

[The Story] Emily Forbes, founder of Seenit, first discovered the potential of collaborative storytelling in South Africa while making a film about rhino conservation protesters. While filming the crowd, she realized she wasn't the only one with a camera in her hands; lots of the protesters were capturing their personal experiences on their smartphones themselves. This raw authenticity inspired Emily to incorporate the wider views into her film.

'Their footage was so much more passionate and opinionated than mine could ever be, so I ran around the crowd asking for their video. I was soon introduced to a wider network and the footage was so impactful. There just needed to be a way to connect the dots to produce a bigger story to get their voices heard,' she said. Emily started to create more video in this way around music festivals and car racing events, selling the content back to the event sponsors. She realized the concept needed to scale. It would be far more efficient if people could upload their videos instantly to a central online platform for her to view and edit. With that, Seenit was born: a video collaboration tool enabling brands and organizations to activate their own customers, experts and employees to become the content creators. In January 2014, Seenit was founded, got support from an accelerator, Collider, and hit the ground running.

[Funding History]

Angel Investment

[Milestones]
- Founding Seenit and raising our first round of funding though the Collider Accelerator
- Bringing on our first subscription client, BBC Earth, in August 2014
- Hitting £1 m in revenue in May 2016
- Watching Seenit content on TV with BT Sport in September 2016

[Links] Website: **seenit.io** Facebook: **Seenit** Twitter: **@_seenit**

[Name] # WeFarm

[Elevator Pitch] *"WeFarm crowd sources vital agricultural information for the 500 million small scale farmers around the world who have no access to the internet."*

[The Story] WeFarm was launched in 2015 by founder and CEO Kenny Ewan, an entrepreneur with a background in international development. After seven years specializing in projects for indigenous communities in Latin America, Kenny returned to the UK in 2014 to work as part of a startup team at the non-governmental organization Cafedirect Producers' Foundation. That's where WeFarm was born. Piloted with farmers in northeast Africa, the WeFarm project grew when the CPF team decided to spin it out as a social business.

The idea was to reach the tens of millions of people in rural parts of the world without access to the internet, those with obvious barriers to basic and essential information on how to battle diseases or plant new crops. WeFarm discovered that the best vehicle for achieving this was SMS text messages. But the platform works in a unique way: instead of simply creating the information it thinks farmers would need and giving it to them, it allows farmers to take advantage of massive scale crowdsourcing, letting people share information and advice as part of a network. So if a farmer in rural Kenya has a problem, a free SMS to WeFarm will be scanned and analyzed by its systems and algorithms until the best people in the network can offer a solution within 24 hours.

[Funding History]

Bootstrap   Seed Funding   Angel Investment

[Milestones]
- Winning the Google impact challenge and finding initial investment
- Obtaining our first 500 real users
- Reaching sustained active monthly engagement, with 30–35 percent of users on the platform six months on
- Hitting 100,000 users, up from 500, in just eighteen months

[Links]   Website: **wefarm.org** Facebook: **wefarmproject** Twitter: **@we_farm**

[Name]
Courier

[Elevator Pitch]
"Courier is a media brand for startups and modern businesses seeking to capture the spirit of transformation in the economy and in society."

[The Story]
Courier came to fruition in 2013 when founder and publisher Jeff Taylor, then a senior client for a large Hong Kong-based conglomerate, met his business partner, future Courier cofounder Soheb Panja, a former journalist who had moved to PR and corporate affairs. The pair were fascinated by the conversations they and their friends were having about businesses and the stories behind them and the increasing interest in the business world coming from regular people.

Inspired by the curious and courageous people they came across who were starting their own ventures in all sorts of sectors, the pair were drawn to the rise of modern business, which they saw as being a million miles from popular interpretations of 'entrepreneurship' seen in TV shows such as Dragons' Den or The Apprentice.

Appalled that there wasn't anything in the business media except news about big corporations and clichéd whiz-kid millionaire tech teenagers, Jeff and Soheb figured there was room in the industry for a media brand that was both authentic and authoritative. In a bid to fill that niche, they set up Courier, a business with a print magazine at its core. Reporting on modern business and startup culture from its headquarters in east London, Courier is now stocked in over 350 outlets in London with a circulation of 50,000.

[Funding History]

Bootstrap

Seed Funding

[Milestones]
- Publishing the first issue in just sixteen weeks
- Receiving the first call from a media agency to spend advertising money
- Closing the first investment round and hitting the target in a few days
- Deciding to launch a regular digital product after successes in print

[Links] Website: **courierpaper.com** Facebook: **Courierpaper** Twitter: **@courierpaper** Instagram: **courierpaper**

[Name] # WiredScore

[Elevator Pitch] *"WiredScore is a connectivity ratings system for commercial real estate, helping landlords benchmark and market the digital connectivity of their buildings to prospective tenants."*

[The Story] WiredScore was founded in 2013 to solve a modern problem: While internet and digital connectivity had become increasingly important to businesses, landlords of well-connected buildings had no way of advertising their connectivity to prospective tenants. Prospective tenants, meanwhile, were often clueless about the quality of a building's internet connectivity when deciding whether or not to move in. With this idea in mind, now cofounder and CEO Arie Barendrecht went to Mayor Bloomberg while working in New York in 2013 and started a company that would rate the digital connectivity of buildings. After seeing immediate success in the Big Apple, Barendrecht didn't waste any time expanding the company to London. Endorsed by the Mayor of London and selected through a competitive process by the Greater London Authority, WiredScore's standards were developed by an advisory board of experts and vetted by key telecom, real estate and tech stakeholders throughout London, creating a recognized measurement now known as Wired Certification.

Launched officially in London in 2015 at the Smart Cities conference, WiredScore has seized on the importance of reliable internet connectivity for business. The company's goal is now to expand internationally – and with big clients wanting to move into Wired Certified buildings, demand shouldn't be a problem.

[Funding History]

Bootstrap

[Milestones]
- Winning a contract to be London's official digital connectivity rating scheme
- Winning the Estates Gazette Rising Stars award
- Launching in Manchester in September 2016, the first UK city outside London
- Hitting 230,000 m² of commercial real estate being certified in London

[Links] Website: **wiredscore.co.uk** Facebook: **WiredScore** Twitter: **@WiredScore**

[Name]

Yoyo Wallet

[Elevator Pitch]

"Yoyo Wallet offers consumers a single mobile payment app that automates the collection of loyalty points and rewards from preferred retailers. Yoyo captures the consumer's basket data, which enables a true personalization of the buying experience."

[The Story]

Yoyo Wallet was founded in May 2013 by Alain Falys, Michael Rolph and Dave Nicolson, all of whom were working in the payments and fintech space and had grown skeptical of the increasing number of payment-only digital wallets. Their breakthrough came when buying coffee via the Starbucks loyalty app one day, which answered the question they'd been circling for months: How do you take mobile payments and harness them into something meaningful for both customers and retailers? The Starbucks experience proved that mobile payment could do more than simply mirror contactless payment; it could deliver payment and rewards in one seamless and personalized experience.

Yoyo Wallet was conceived with the vision that mobile payments had the potential to redefine a whole industry. The team created a prototype which achieved four goals: delivering fast and secure mobile payment, creating some form of reward for the user with every purchase, becoming a single destination that housed multiple brands and helping retailers better understand their customers' behaviors and preferences. The company struck a deal with over sixty universities around the UK, and shortly afterwards they rolled out to corporate environments, eventually launching in 150 businesses such as Accenture, M&C Saatchi and The Hilton. With its latest sign ups, including Planet Organic and Caffè Nero, Yoyo Wallet is rapidly growing in the consumer retail space.

[Funding History]

Angel Investment

Venture Capital

[Milestones]

- Rolling out a beta version of the app at Imperial College, London in Nov 2013
- Becoming Europe's fastest growing mobile wallet app by Apr 2015
- Going live in over 50 percent of UK universities and over 150 corporate locations by Sep 2016
- Being selected by Caffè Nero in autumn 2016 for their 613 UK and Ireland stores

[Links]   Website: **yoyowallet.com** Facebook: **yoyowallet** Twitter: **@Yoyowallet** Instagram: **yoyo_wallet**

[Name]
PROPERCORN

[Elevator Pitch]
"PROPERCORN is healthy popcorn done properly. But we also go further: we mentor small businesses, make clothes, collaborate with young, creative talent and place a huge emphasis on enjoying what we do."

[The Story]
PROPERCORN cofounder and CEO Cassandra Stavrou always had a dream of setting up her own company, an 'entrepreneurial itch' as she calls it. This is what spurred her on to quit her day job at an advertising agency in 2009, aged twenty-five, and follow her dream to build a business and create a healthy snack that was both satisfying and delicious. It was also important to grow an exciting and dynamic brand, 'a healthy snack that people would be proud to be seen with.'

With this vision, Cassandra moved back home and worked in a pub on evenings and weekends to save £10,000 to get things up and running. She also used the time to learn business basics through a free course at East London's small business center, looked into designs for branding and experimented with novel ways of seasoning popcorn. She had to be resourceful: she acquired a cement mixer, lined it with steel and ordered a car spraying kit to apply oil in a fine mist, and that's how the first batches were made. 'I was a young girl with almost no experience, so getting people to take me seriously was a challenge,' Cassandra says, but after two years of hard graft, she found a manufacturer and launched PROPERCORN in 2010 with best friend and business partner Ryan Kohn. Both still work with the same factory today.

[Funding History]

Bootstrap

Seed Funding

[Milestones]
- Figuring out how to successfully season the popcorn using a cement mixer
- Coming together with Ryan and forming a perfect working relationship
- Making Google the first big customer
- Moving into the first PROPERCORN headquarters

[Links]   Website: propercorn.com   Facebook: Propercorn   Twitter: @Propercorn   Instagram: propercorn

[Name] # Jukedeck

[Elevator Pitch] *"Jukedeck is an artificially intelligent music composer – software that writes original pieces completely on its own, helping video creators find music for their videos that is unique, royalty free and customizable at the touch of a button."*

[The Story] Jukedeck was created after founder and CEO Ed Rex stumbled into a computer science lecture while visiting his girlfriend at Harvard University in 2012. Astounded by what he discovered, Ed decided to teach himself computer programming.

Knowing little about technology but a lot about music, Ed's newfound interest in computer science spurred him to revisit a question he'd had while studying at Cambridge University: Whether it would be possible for computers to write music. A published composer himself, Ed brought his composition expertise and married it to his new programming skills, and it wasn't long before he began to write the first algorithms that would later make Jukedeck.

Several months after working on his musical algorithms, Ed reached out to childhood friend (and now cofounder and COO) Patrick Stobbs for help. Impressed by Ed's achievements, Stobbs, who was working at Google at the time, immediately saw what he describes as "a significant opportunity" in the idea – to provide music for all kinds of people that really struggle to find music for their projects. The pair joined forces, and Jukedeck was born, a system that learns how to write music, chord by chord and note by note.

[Funding History]

Bootstrap   Seed Funding   Venture Capital

[Milestones]
- The first time the Jukedeck system successfully played music
- When someone first used the software for a video game
- Launching at TechCrunch Disrupt and winning the competition, resulting in 40,000 signups
- Being awarded a Cannes Lion in 2016; receiving validation from the advertising community

[Links]   Website: **jukedeck.com** Facebook: **jukedeck** Twitter: **@Jukedeck** Instagram: **jukedeck**

- **The big picture**
  For a successful beginning, a startup should consider building a business that venture capital can invest in – one that is looking to scale globally.

- **The right team**
  When expanding the team, look for relevant people with the experience and skillset to execute their idea in a fresh way, rather than using solutions already in the market.

- **The right market**
  Look to scale in a market big enough to sell to via a bottom-up approach.

- **Know your customer**
  Have a clear definition of who your customer is, and an understanding of the value you bring to that customer.

- **A drive to test their assumptions**
  Validate data; assume you don't know everything

- **Willingness**
  You should want to seek advice and listen. This doesn't mean you have to execute every bit of advice you hear – make your own decisions but be open to new insight.

[Name]

Wayra UK

[Elevator Pitch]

"Wayra UK is part of Telefónica Open Future_, the open program that integrates the different initiatives of the whole Telefónica Group related to entrepreneurship and innovation."

[Sector]

Digital, Technology

[Description]

Wayra UK gives direct funding, acceleration and pre-acceleration services, such as coworking spaces, mentoring, access to Wayra UK's network and knowhow, training in entrepreneurship and business skills to selected startups. The accelerator was started in Latin America and Spain in 2011 as an initiative of Telefónica's chief executive in Europe, José María Álvarez-Pallete. By 2013, there were fourteen Wayra academies in twelve countries in Europe and Latin America. Since its launch in the UK in 2012, Wayra UK startups have raised over US$100 m in third-party investment.

In a bid to help generate growth, create a positive impact on society and fuel innovation across a number of industries, Wayra UK has partnered with some of the world's leading organizations in fashion, health and cyber security industries to offer accelerator programs for a variety of startups. One example is Merck Sharp & Dohme Limited (MSD), a global company transforming healthcare. Coming together to launch a partnership called Velocity Health, the teams will aid healthcare startups, ensuring they get access to Merck's expertise and networks. The goal is to help accelerate the startups in identifying new and sustainable ways of delivering patient care, both now and in the future. Wayra UK has also partnered with online fashion house ASOS to find and nurture fashion technology startups, giving them access to relevant networks and support. The idea is to develop technology that will give fashion startups a platform to grow. In addition, GCHQ is also working with Wayra UK to nurture the next generation of cyber security startups and make the online world a safer place.

The accelerator is on the lookout for digital and tech startups to join its main program in London, as well as for its Open Future_ programs in Birmingham and Oldham.

[Apply to]

wayra.co.uk

[Links]   Website: **wayra.co.uk** Facebook: **wayra.org** Twitter: **@Wayra**

- **Strive for impact**
  The most attractive startups are ones that do something big, whether that's disrupting a market, solving an issue that affects millions or saving lives. Put in the hours to make something amazing.

- **Find the right match**
  There are a lot of accelerators out there, but not all will be helpful for your company. Take the time to do your research, and reach out to alumni in order to find the best fit for you and your startup.

- **Express your passion**
  The community will feed off your passion for your idea. Communicate this in your networking, marketing and pitches, and the audience will recognize your commitment to the idea and its potential for success.

- **Know your facts**
  Know your industry and market inside and out. Become an expert in your specific area and you'll be able to spot trends and opportunities ahead of others.

[Name]

MassChallenge UK

[Elevator Pitch]

"No equity and not-for-profit, MassChallenge UK is obsessed with helping promising entrepreneurs from all industries. Our highest-impact startups are rewarded through a competition to win a portion of equity-free cash awards."

[Sector]

Agnostic

[Description]

Through a global network of accelerators in Boston, the UK, Israel, Switzerland and Mexico, MassChallenge UK connects high-impact, early-stage startups with mentors, partners and investors, while providing what it calls "high-impact support" during a three-month accelerator program. The accelerator believes it can have a massive impact in driving growth and creating value all over the world. And it seems to be well on track to doing just that. Since 2010, over one thousand MassChallenge UK alumni have raised over £1.4 billion, generated over £500 m in revenue and created over 60,000 jobs. Startups supported by MassChallenge UK have access to an extensive global network that draws on experts from the community and offers connections to over 100 top corporate partners including Nestle, Proctor & Gamble, Microsoft, IBM and The Boston Consulting Group. There's also a plethora of workshops on offer in its office space, designed to build the skill sets of entrepreneurs and prepare them to grow their startups.

'We look for high-impact startups that are disrupting an industry, creating jobs, saving lives or solving a major problem, as well as startups with high potential that have a cogent vision for their company's growth,' says CMO Diane Perlman. Its application process opens every spring, and looks for early-stage startups – that's any startup that's raised less than £300,000 of investment and has less than £600,000 in annual revenue – in any industry, from anywhere in the world.

Diane suggests that younger startups reach out to their local ecosystem for help. 'Do your research, and find the support resources that best fit your company vision. Take care to maintain a healthy balance between work and life. Many people can get burned out by their work by letting it consume their life.'

[Apply to]

masschallenge.org

- **Be bold and ambitious**
Look to tackle global problems. It's important to dream big, no matter what stage the business is at.

- **Be crystal clear with your mission**
Make your business mission front and center of what you do. The powerful thing about startups is that they are agile and can quickly adapt to changing situations – but having a strong purpose and mission from the start will encourage others to buy into what you're doing.

- **Attend networking and industry events**
Be on the lookout for accelerator programs, speak to everyone and get networking. Attend events, conferences and meetups. Being around like-minded people opens up opportunities.

- **Learn from mentors**
Listen to people who have trodden a similar path – serial entrepreneurs and those who have been through the ups and downs of entrepreneurism themselves. These people have invaluable advice and often share it for free.

Level39

[Name]

[Elevator Pitch]

"Level39 is an accelerator space where tenants of Canary Wharf and elsewhere can bring about innovation; a space where entrepreneurs are tackling the world's most valuable opportunities."

[Sector]

Fintech, Cyber Security, Retail Technology, Smart City Technology

[Description]

Taking up three floors of the tallest skyscraper in London's financial district, Level39 is a tech accelerator space located on level 24, 42 and – you guessed it – 39 at One Canada Square, Canary Wharf, surrounded by some of the world's largest institutions. Wholly owned by the Canary Wharf Group, Level39 launched in March 2013. Since then, it has grown from a simple idea into a 7,500 m^2 accelerator space dedicated to implementing innovation and giving businesses the room to grow, whether they're made up of four people or forty people. With its entrepreneurs tackling the world's most valuable opportunities in sectors including financial technology, cyber security, retail technology and smart cities, there are 180 startups working inside – approximately 800 people.

The Level39 team works with corporate partners and international organizations, investors and government bodies to help businesses across all sectors. The majority of its members are early-stage startups. Those looking to apply can do so via a simple application online or through a network of referrals. They then have a two-stage interview with Level39's memberships team who try to identify potential applicants and, if satisfied, bring them on board to join the Level39 family.

There's also the High Growth Space, which occupies the entire 42nd floor, covering 2690 m^2. This was launched to meet the demand of technology companies, including graduates from Level39 and its accelerator programs. Through a tailored curriculum, expert mentors, a packed events calendar and high-end facilities, Level39 has helped entrepreneurs turn simple products into multimillion pound businesses.

[Apply to]

Level39 Ecosystem Team / **members@level39.co**

- **Have the right team in place**
  In any startup the key is the team. The team members should have diverse skillsets, be passionate about the business and be able to adapt quickly.

- **Perfect your story**
  Every founder should be able to tell their story in an engaging and concise manner. This does not mean using technical language or talking in metrics, but rather articulating your "aha" moment and the reason you're solving a problem.

- **Find the right product market fit**
  Never assume your business will be able to disrupt an existing market. Talk to customers, use data and constantly optimize.

- **Focus on getting customers**
  Without customers, your startup is just an idea. Customers enable you to validate and find the right product-market fit, prove the investment worthiness of your idea and, of course, help you generate an income.

[Name]
Startupbootcamp

[Elevator Pitch]
"Startupbootcamp is a family of fifteen industry-focused programs that support startups with direct access to an international network of the most relevant mentors, partners and investors to help them scale globally."

[Sector]
Fintech, Insurtech, IoT-connected Devices

[Description]
Originally founded in Copenhagen, Startupbootcamp made its home in London in 2013 and has been headquartered there ever since. The organization comprises 15 accelerator programs in 10 cities across 3 continents, investing in more than 350 startups from more than 30 countries, making it the largest early-stage investor outside of the US. Each of Startupbootcamp's programs invests in specific industries; for example, fintech, Internet of Things, smart cities, foodtech and e-commerce. Due to this deeper industry focus, Startupbootcamp is able to provide startups with hands-on support and access to connections that matter most in the startup's industry.

Startupbootcamp's programs are open to startups worldwide. Receiving hundreds of applications per program, they invest in the top ten teams for each. 'We accelerate a variety of startups at different stages and industries,' says the company's head of global, Andrew Shannon. 'Typically the early-stage startups entering our program have a core team with diverse skillsets in place, and a product built that initial customers are using.'

The programs run for three months, and allow startups to meet over 100 partners, investors and mentors who take a hands-on role in helping the company develop their product, validate their business model, secure pilot customers and raise funding. In addition, each startup receives €15,000 in cash, €450,000 in partner services and four months of free collaborative office space. In return for these program benefits, Startupbootcamp asks for between 6 and 8 percent equity. The support doesn't end after the three intense months of acceleration. Startupbootcamp believes this is just the beginning of a long-term partnership where they work closely with the startup as they scale their company.

[Apply to]
startupbootcamp.org

[Links] Facebook: **startupbootcamp** Twitter: **@Sbootcamp** Instagram: **startupbootcamp**

- **Be prepared for long sales cycles**
  Sales cycles for larger corporate organizations take much longer for cyber security solutions, so be aware of this when planning your strategy.

- **Don't neglect the end-user experience**
  For your product to be effective the user should not have to drastically change their processes and habits in order to be more secure. This is vital in order to maximize adoption of cyber security best practice.

- **Make it as easy as possible for your solution to be adopted**
  Minimize deployment complexity and technical integration for your users. The simpler the integration process, the more likely clients will run pilots and proof of concepts.

- **Make sure you're really solving a problem**
  Focus carefully on sales and commercial commitments before going far beyond an MVP of your solution. Feedback on your initial product is vital, and you will only get this if you get out and test it with customers.

CyLon

[Name]

[Elevator Pitch]

"CyLon offers entrepreneurs the platform they need to build and grow a successful cyber security company. Its three-month program offers a tailored professional curriculum, and support from an accomplished network of mentors."

[Sector]

Cyber Security: Defense, Retail, Telecoms, Fintech, Digital Media, Health Services

[Description]

Founded by leading security, investment and policy experts, CyLon is a cyber security accelerator offering entrepreneurs the training necessary for building and growing a successful cyber security company. Each of the participating startups receives funding, training and connections as part of their membership, and it concludes with a Demo Day, where the teams present to a wide range of leading industry partners and investors.

CyLon invests £15,000 in each team, in return for a 3 percent equity stake. It believes this funding allows the startup teams to fully commit to the three-month program and focus on building their technology and company. As part of this, they are introduced to a variety of other investors throughout the program, giving them the opportunity to pitch for further funding. The program offers an intensive training curriculum that covers the challenges and opportunities encountered by early-stage cyber security companies, helping them to achieve product-market fit in a uniquely technical and demanding industry. The curriculum includes everything from business fundamentals and recruitment to product pricing and technical training.

CyLon prides itself in offering key connections for startups. During the program, it invites leading industry and government figures to speak to participating companies, arranges business development trips and introduces potential partners and clients. During the course of the program, all teams are based in CyLon's London office, provided by Winton Capital. There are no formal restrictions concerning a company's stage or size, and applications from small teams with big ambitions are welcome. 'We accept teams from all over the world, but expect founders to participate in person, in London, for the duration of the program,' says program director Katie Bilton. 'Some of our alumni include Ripjar, SQR Systems, CheckRecipient and Sphere.'

[Apply to]

Katie Bilton / katie@cylonlan.com

[Links]

Website: **cylonlab.com** Twitter: **@CylonLab**

- **Know your fellow founders**
  Founders who know their cofounders tend to have longer relationships and a better understanding of each other during the tough times that will follow.

- **Start from your experience**
  Start a company from your own (negative) experience, when you want to improve some thing's current state. You can relate to the challenge easier, see the solution faster and be more passionate about it.

- **Ask people if they need your product or service**
  Before spending months on building your business, do some customer research. Don't be so sure that everyone has the same need as you.

- **An in-house tech team is important**
  Due to the constant product iterations and improvements that will be necessary, having an in-house tech team and understanding can be crucial.

- **Clean cap table**
  A majority of companies will need to fundraise. Having a fair and clean cap table where everyone is content with their position can make a difference.

[Name]
Techstars

[Elevator Pitch]
"Techstars is a global ecosystem that empowers entrepreneurs to bring new technologies to market. With dozens of mentorship-driven accelerator programs and thousands of startup programs worldwide, Techstars exists to support entrepreneurs throughout their lifelong journey, from inspiration to IPO."

[Sector]
Technology; Web and Software

[Description]
Techstars funds technology-oriented companies, typically web and software-based – and usually ones that are a little outside the norm. They're always on the lookout for companies that can have national or worldwide reach.

The startup accelerator and development program came about thanks to serial entrepreneurs David Cohen and David Brown. After building successful businesses themselves, the pair decided to help other entrepreneurs. At first, they invited a bunch of companies to meet some other people, such as mentors, who would give them advice and suggestions around their businesses. They put some structure around it, created a three-month program and got it up and running, and in 2006, Techstars was born. Ten years later, that company has roughly twenty-five accelerator programs, 7,000 founders, mentors, investors and corporate partners, and more than 8,000 community leaders who work together to create a worldwide network of entrepreneurial support. Techstars launched Techstars London in 2013, the first international Techstars location outside the US. Home to a thriving international community of tech, founders, innovators and investors, Techstars believes London is an epicenter of startup activity. Applications for the first cohort in London were four times greater than in previous years, totaling 1,302 applications from 72 different countries.

'We've done five programs so far with more than fifty companies going through it – from artificial intelligence and database startups to fintech, FOG-tech (fat-oil-grease) and aid,' says managing director of Techstars London Max Kelly. 'Usually, the group of companies is very international, with the most recent cohort having nineteen nationalities for roughly forty-five people.' Techstars thinks that the value of learning, networking and mentoring provided by the program is its greatest benefit, and promises to provide startups with what it calls 'the healthiest possible start' and greatly improve a company's chances for success and sustainability.

[Apply to]
Marko Srsan / **marko.srsan:techstars.com**

[Links]
Website: **techstars.com** Twitter: **@techstars**

- Don't keep your ideas secret
  Many people have great ideas but won't tell
  anyone, either because they're too afraid to share
  their ideas or are afraid someone will steal them.
  But they won't get help or mentoring this way.

- Social and intellectual capital are key
  Don't assume money is the first step to building a
  business: your networks and your knowledge are
  the first things you should strive for, and the
  money will come later.

- Avoid tech jargon
  There's a lot of tech jargon pollution in business
  ideas. Don't get distracted by tech babble – focus
  on the main things, like selling your product.

- Open up
  Don't be afraid to show that you're vulnerable or
  don't know something. It's easy to bottle things
  up and want to abandon ship, but instead, get
  advice from those with experience.

Launch22

[Name]

[Elevator Pitch]

"Launch22 is a charity incubator aimed at helping startups and entre-
preneurs get off the ground, regardless of the business they are starting.
We offer subsidized workspaces, mentoring, events and a community in
a more rounded ecosystem than other tech-focused incubators."

[Sector]

Agnostic: Tech, Charity, Design and Product Businesses

[Description]

'If you come to us as a startup, you not only get a home but you get the help of others,'
says Launch22 founder Eddie Holmes, who has been an entrepreneur himself since he
was sixteen. Eddie set up Launch22 in 2014 to create a place for those looking to get
their businesses off the ground, find peer support and get access to good advice. Run
by Eddie and center manager Tom Previte – and with the help of several volunteers
– the team is dedicated to helping entrepreneurs and businesses feel welcome in the
space. 'We believe that access to business support services should be available to
everyone no matter what your background or starting point is,' says Eddie. 'Whether
you are setting up a barber shop, an accountancy practice or aiming to disrupt an
industry with a purely digital offering, we are a home for you.'

Launch22 is just minutes from Old Street station. It keeps its prices low to be ap-
proachable for anyone beginning their journey of entrepreneurship, and as part of a
scholarship program, provides 30 percent of the incubator's space for free to those
from underrepresented or underprivileged backgrounds. They offer a fully serviced
workspace (with in-house dogs included), on-site mentoring and all manner of startup
events. They also provide internships to students in event management and marketing. Pricing for desk space is very competitive, starting from just £55 per month plus
VAT, rising to £260 for a fixed desk space with all day access and unlimited access
to mentors. At night, Launch22 turns into a multipurpose event space, with different
groups hosting events and workshops amidst its very own signature events, Speed
Networking, Entrepreneurs Anonymous and Fireside Chat, to name a few.

[Apply to]

Eddie Holmes / info@launch22.co.uk

ces

[Name] Future Cities Catapult

[Address]   1 Sekforde St, London, EC1R 0BE

✕ Future Cities Catapult

LONDON

[Total Area]

331M²

[Workspaces]

5

[The Story]   Stationed in London's Urban Innovation Centre, Future Cities Catapult provides facilities and expertise to support small to medium enterprises (SMEs), the development of new products and services, as well as opportunities to collaborate with others, test ideas and develop business models. It's geared towards helping innovators to discuss, engage and cocreate the next generation of integrated urban systems. The center features spacious clean white walls which are punctutated nicely with large windows that give a glimpse into the leafy surroundings of Clerkenwell.

The center's third floor has recently been opened up as a coworking space via Catapult Carnet, a new scheme that welcomes future city-related SMEs and grants members access to hot-desking, ideal for those working in the innovation and cities sectors that need occasional use of a Central London office space. After a one-off joining fee of £50, members can purchase a carnet, which is a package of ten tickets for £250 plus VAT. Each ticket allows access to a desk in the coworking space for one day or two half days, Monday to Friday. To attract budding entrepreneurs and startups, Future Cities Catapult also has a mini coworking space of five desks located alongside resident innovators.

[Links]   Website: **futurecities.catapult.org.uk** Facebook: **Future-Cities-Catapult-Urban-Innovation-Centre**

Face of the Space:
Gemma Guilera is Future Cities Catapult's
SME program lead, tasked with providing
the small businesses with the tools and
network connections they need to
transform the future of cities.

[Name] # Interchange

[Address]   Interchange Triangle, Chalk Farm Rd, London NW1 8AB

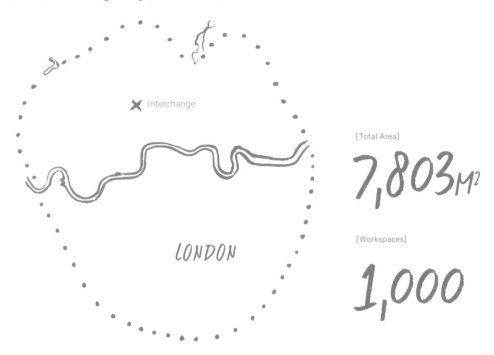

Interchange

LONDON

[Total Area]

7,803M²

[Workspaces]

1,000

[The Story]   Designed from top to bottom by Design Research Studio under the supervision of Tom Dixon, Interchange is perhaps one of London's most flashy coworking spaces. Bespoke desks and chairs offer members not only a unique place to set up camp, but also a view through floor-to-ceiling windows across Camden and beyond to the skyscrapers of the city and Canary Wharf. The space brings a minimalist Scandinavian feel to what was once one of London's historic centers of trade, situated next to the Regents Canal. And it doesn't just look great – Interchange's facilities give members access to a full kitchen, gym and restaurant. It's got a small community library, too, where books can be borrowed from a collection curated specifically for startups. Those looking for some audit, tax and advisory services can simply pop in to see KPMG, which has a residency there.

Those needing a break from the computer screen can escape to one of many outdoor balcony spaces for those rare occasions when London decides to shine, to a peaceful retreat from the buzz of Camden Market below. With three locations sitting side-by-side, and open 24/7, Interchange starts from £40 per day, £100 per month on a flexi plan or £450 for a fixed desk.

[Links]   Website: interchange.io Facebook: interchangeLDN Twitter: @interchangeLDN

Face of the Space:

Katie Clarke, operations manager at Interchange, is a true Londoner. Growing up in the Southeast of the city, her passion and real love for startup culture grew from her previous role working for a company that helped incubate and mentor entre-preneurs and small businesses, giving her the chance to see them grow from one- or two-person businesses to big teams.

[Name]

TechHub

[Address]   TechHub, 20 Ropemaker St, London EC2Y 9AR, UK

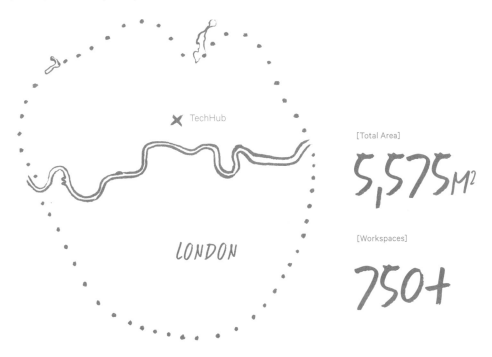

TechHub

LONDON

[Total Area]

5,575M²

[Workspaces]

750+

[The Story]   Not every coworking space has a karaoke bar, but this is just one of many things that make TechHub a unique space for tech entrepreneurs and startups in central London. The idea for TechHub emerged when founder and CEO Elizabeth Varley was brainstorming ideas for creating a space where startups and entrepreneurs could collaborate, access space and advice and help each other. Launched in 2010, the community now has more than 750 startups globally across Europe and India and 60 nationalities beavering away under its London roof. 'Our team is very multinational, which helps you feel you're part of the global tech phenomenon,' says Elizabeth, adding that the community's international outlook is exactly what helps companies go global. Built exclusively for product tech companies, TechHub gives members access to their full program and opportunities, no matter which level of membership they take. Prices start at £425 +VAT per year for a flexible membership, with drop-in access to the space. Those wanting a 24/7 membership can become resident members from £275 +VAT per month with 24/7 access. 'What we think is really unique is our community, which is exclusively made up of entrepreneurs and startup teams going through the same challenges, is there's significant peer-to-peer support.'

[Links]   Website: **techhub.com** Facebook: **TechHub** Twitter: **@TechHub** Instagram: **techhublondon**

Face of the Space:
Founder and CEO of TechHub Elizabeth Varley is a serial entrepreneur with a background in communications and community. Her career began as a writer, editor and later content strategist, which led her to running a successful editorial agency. However, it was her love of community and bringing people together that led her to set up what is now one of London's biggest coworking spaces.

[Name]   # The Collective

[Address]   14 Bedford Square, Fitzrovia, London WC1B 3JA

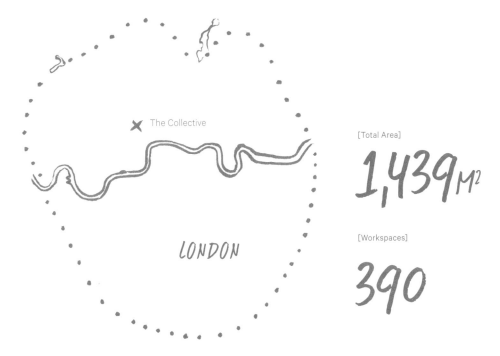

The Collective

LONDON

[Total Area]

1,439M²

[Workspaces]

390

[The Story]   The Collective's spaces aren't just dedicated to coworking – it has a groundbreaking 'coliving' property too. Its coliving model combines the convenience and community of a boutique hotel with the community of a student dormitory, just without the beans on toast and freshman parties. With the goal of 'offering a way of living focused on a genuine sense of community,' The Collective offers shared spaces and facilities in the same place to foster a modern, appealing lifestyle.

In 2014 The Collective Bedford Square opened, a coworking space built on the realization that the boundaries between work and play are becoming more blurred. It creates an unparalleled work environment for its teams, and has enough space to ensure they're surrounded by other cutting edge start ups. The Collective is now a company of over fifty people and has just launched its seventh space in West London – The Collective Old Oak – which it is calling 'the world's largest coliving building.' The space features communal entertainment spaces, luxury facilities and dining rooms for private and social events. Your rent, bills, utilities and taxes are all taken care of in a simple monthly fee. With a dedicated concierge service on hand 24/7, there's nothing you'll need that The Collective hasn't already thought of.

[Links]   Website: **thecollective.co.uk** Facebook: **CollectiveOrg** Twitter: **@collective_llp**

Face of the Space:

Property entrepreneur Reza Merchant, the founder and CEO of The Collective, set up the space while studying at university in 2010. 'The Collective is an environment where members can spend lots of time and have lots of great events going on. We didn't want it to feel like an office; it's partly an office, partly a home and partly a nightclub,' he says.

[Name] # Rainmaking Loft

[Address] International House, 1 St Katharine's Way, London E1W 1UN

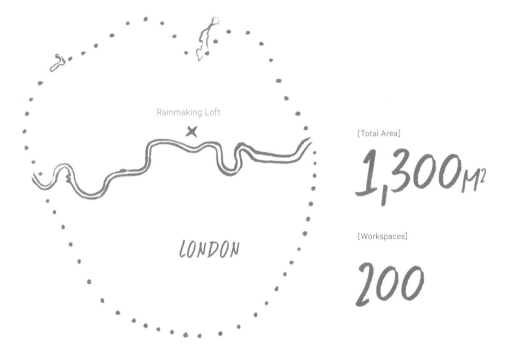

Rainmaking Loft

LONDON

[Total Area]

1,300M²

[Workspaces]

200

[The Story] Set within the peaceful St. Katharine Docks marina and made all the more alluring by a floating meeting room and views of classic London landmarks, this not-for-profit coworking space is the first of its kind in the Tower Bridge area. Called Rainmaking Loft, the space is part of the Rainmaking group, a brand born from a collection of entrepreneurs from Denmark. Opening its first coworking space in London in 2013, Rainmaking Loft was born with the desire to create a supportive community for the multiple Rainmaking startups in one flexible office space.

The space was bigger than needed, and thus the Rainmaking group invited other London-based startups to collaborate alongside them, making for an organic co-working concept under one roof. Rainmaking is now focused on community as a foundation for being a major player in the London Startup ecosystem, and a launchpad for young businesses. Not just about technology, the space is open to startups or entrepreneurs that offer something to the community in terms of enthusiasm, energy and entrepreneurial spirit. 'We're not restrictive on who we allow to work here,' says general manager Jane Campbell. 'As long as we feel the community fit is right; and that the startup is interested in engaging within a collaborative space.'

[Links] Website: rainmakingloft.com Facebook: rainmakingloft Twitter: @RainmakingLoft

Face of the Space:

General manager Jane Campbell managed a digital product studio in Shoreditch for six years previous to her role at Rainmaking Loft. Witnessing it grow into a global success story made her want to play a bigger part in the early stages of a startup journey. 'I believe in the community spirit of Rainmaking Loft, the ethos of the space we run and the diversity of companies it attracts,' she says.

[Name] # TMRW

[Address] 75-77 High St, Croydon CR0 1QQ

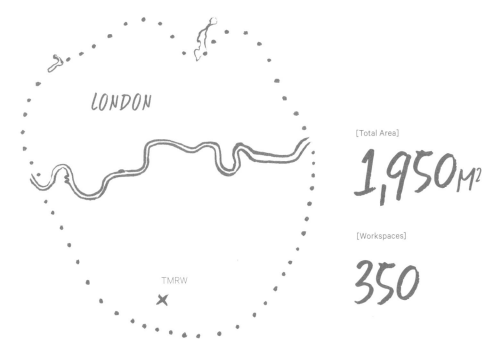

LONDON

TMRW

[Total Area]

1,950M²

[Workspaces]

350

[The Story] Located nine miles out of the city, in Croydon, TMRW is the latest hotspot for tech startups in South London and prides itself in being more spacious than – and costing half the price of – centrally-located coworking spaces.

Wide office space stretches as far as the eye can see, punctuated by large bespoke desks, giving members room to breathe and work without limitations. Private offices line the walls on either side. TMRW's spacious theme continues with its hip graffiti-strewn events area, which can host 350 people, with the same number of coworking desks and dedicated desks available.

GigaBit internet and wifi flow throughout, made all the better by an adjoining café that promises to serve up the best coffee in town, as well as a (free) 3D printing lab. TMRW's mission is 'to build a credible tech city, where the greats from tech can find, work with, invest in and assist promising fast-growth companies in achieving their dreams,' and with a space like this, you won't doubt it.

[Links] Website: **tmrw.co** Facebook: **tmrwhub** Twitter: **@tmrwhub** Instagram: **tmrwhub**

Face of the Space:

When he's not building, advising and financing tech companies, François Mazoudier, founder and chairman of TMRW, runs Tech Leaders Capital, a coinvestment club for global tech CEOs. He previously worked in executive roles building technology companies, and experienced the great highs of a startup-to-Nasdaq IPO run and the lows of a total-wipeout bankruptcy – so he definitely knows the score when it comes to the rollercoaster world of tech startups.

[Name] # Here East

[Address] Here East Press Centre, Queen Elizabeth Olympic Park, London, E20 3BS

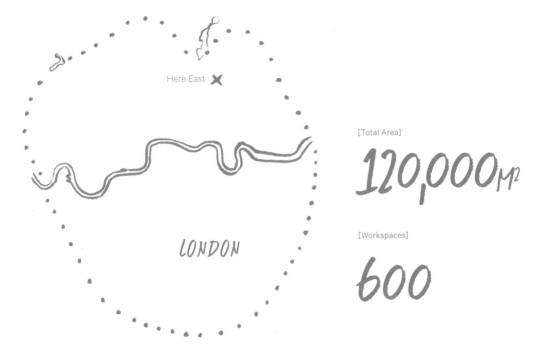

Here East ✕

LONDON

[Total Area]
120,000 M²

[Workspaces]
600

[The Story] Here East is a campus on a scale few can compete with in London. It sits in the lush grounds of the Olympic Park, and it's one of the largest coworking spaces in the capital, stretching over 100,000 m², boasting unparalleled infrastructure made out of the technological capabilities of the London 2012 Olympic Press and Broadcast Centre.

Following a stripped-back theme with natural woods and playful colors dotted in between, Here East prides itself as 'London's home for making, and a unique environment for collaboration and innovation'. It's a digital hub on a huge scale; a place where startups can share expertise with a range of businesses growing in scale, including education institutions and creative organizations. Here East provides versatile spaces with access to power and data at competitive prices for the UK's creative and digital industries, including shared workspaces, a landscaped canal side and independent cafes, shops and restaurants that form an essential part of the Here East community. At the heart of all this is Plexal, an innovation ecosystem claiming to be the largest in Europe. Plexal offers support services that it believes can accelerate growth, empower businesses to scale and weave a legacy.

[Links] Website: **hereeast.com** Facebook: **HereEastLondon** Twitter: @HereEast Instagram: **Hereeast**

Face of the Space:

Gavin Poole is the CEO of Here East, responsible for delivering the overall vision of the space and ensuring the right mix of big and small companies, universities and creative organizations come together, share ideas and collaborate.

[Name] # WeWork

[Address]   Paddington, 2 Eastbourne Terrace, London, W2 6LG

WeWork

LONDON

[Total Area]

65,000+M²

[Workspaces]

12,000

[The Story]   When Richard Branson popped into the Moorgate office of WeWork a few months ago, he wasn't after a desk – the Virgin entrepreneur had been invited to share his thoughts on education as part of a series of WeWork events. The flexible office business, founded in 2010 by Miguel McKelvey, Adam Neumann and Rebekah Neumann has more than 100 locations worldwide and a US$16 billion valuation. Drop-in membership starts at US$45 a month, and it also offers hot desking from around US$250 a month, dedicated desks and private offices. 'WeWork is for people who don't just work to make a living, but a life,' says managing director Eugen Miropolski. 'We have a community of creators. You might see a person in T-shirt and jeans next to a sixty-year-old in shirt and tie, looking at a computer together: people learn from each other.'

In the swish seven-story Paddington office, there are kitchens on every floor, two terraces, quiet rooms for phone calls, larger spaces and private offices. Each location has unique touches: here, it is hundreds of unique, hand-painted tiles leading down to the basement games room and social space. But WeWork members everywhere can take advantage of the "WE" social network, and – at the end of a tough creative day – beer taps brimming with free, local brew.

[Links]   Website: wework.com/l/london Facebook: WeWork Twitter: @WeWork Instagram: wework

Face of the Space:
Eugen Miropolski, the 29-year-old
managing director of WeWork Europe
and Israel, joined eighteen months ago,
and is now in charge of fouteen London
offices (two being built). He likes to look
through the glass walls of the Paddington
site to see conversations happening.
'We want ideal locations and an
environment that fosters energy and
creativity,' he says.

Central Working

[Name]

[Address]   2 Kingdom St, London W2 6BD

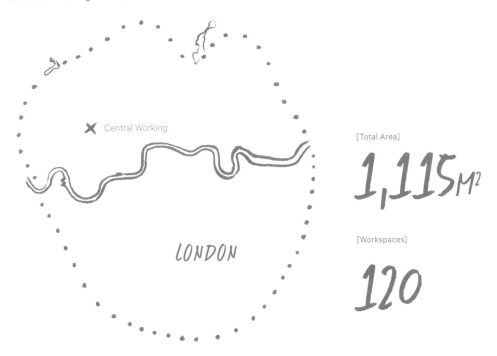

Central Working

LONDON

[Total Area]

1,115M²

[Workspaces]

120

[The Story]   The term 'coworking' didn't really exist when Central Working first launched back in 2011, but the company has come a long way since then, and now has six London spaces, the newest in Paddington.

Founded by James Layfield after building a business managing an airport lounge in JFK, Central Working was conceived as a result of trips to and from New York. Desperate for somewhere decent to work that was quiet and had everything an office has, James thought, 'What if we stick an airport lounge in the city centre?' This formed the basis of Central Working: somewhere hospitality-focused with a support network of like-minded people that encourages communication.

Central Working's Paddington location brings a natural, homely feel to what would otherwise be a void in the core of the corporate office environment at 2 Kingdom Street. The open-plan club features a fifty-person auditorium, several meeting spaces and an independant coffee shop. Central Working is 'fundamentally agnostic' says James, open to anyone passionate about what they do. 'The space attracts all kinds of fast growth businesses, from people in marketing, fashion design and everything in between.'

[Links]   Website: **centralworking.com** Facebook: **centralworking** Twitter: **@centralworking**

Face of the Space:

James Layfield is a serial entrepreneur who started out in advertising working with brands such as Absolut Vodka, Sony Playstation and Virgin. After setting up Escape Airports Ltd at JFK and transforming it from a failing venture to a success, James set his sights on his coworking project, which later became Central Working. He was named a London Technology Ambassador by the Mayor of London, in 2015.

[Name] # Techspace

[Address]   32-38 Leman Street, E1 8EW

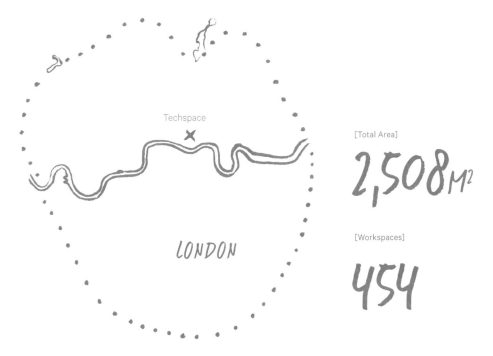

Techspace

LONDON

[Total Area]

2,508M²

[Workspaces]

454

[The Story]   Six airy floors of office space filled with natural light and topped off by a roof terrace make up the Techspace coworking space in Aldgate East, the newest location of five different hubs under the same name. Sitting between the City and London's tech district, Techspace is a community organization created to help technology companies bridge the gap from startup to scale-up. Its chief commercial officer, Philip Ellis, believes that this sense of community – along with the opportunity for larger members to customize the space and make it their own – is the organization's main differentiator.

'We allow companies to brand their own space, and we've actually productized this process in order to offer more flexibility to the members,' says Philip. This, along with bike storage, free meeting rooms, 24 hour access and self-contained floors on demand, means that companies at Techspace can feel more ownership of the space, something Phil says other coworking spaces in London don't currently offer. Sitting at the edge of Shoreditch, Techspace boasts a wealth of local charm, with cafes, bars and restaurants on the doorstep. With the likes of Uber, General Assembly and Unruly Media making their HQs in the same area, it's fast becoming the next tech hub in East London.

[Links]   Website: **Techspace.co** Facebook: **techspaceco** Twitter: **@techspaceco**

Face of the Space:

Philip Ellis is one of the founding partners at Techspace, looking after Marketing, Memberships and Community. 'Managing a community at scale is challenging, but Techspace is a growth business too, so it's helpful to be a part of a community we can also learn from,' he says.

[Name] # Runway East

[Address] Lower Ground, 10 Finsbury Square, London EC2A 1AF

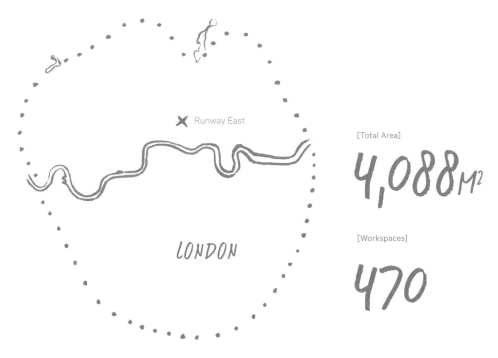

Runway East

LONDON

[Total Area]

4,088m²

[Workspaces]

470

[The Story] A mini-golf course emerges like an island in a sea of desks. Runway East is a coworking space that doesn't take itself too seriously, instead taking pride in being a place where people feel they can be comfortable with their peers and be honest. 'Startup life is a rollercoaster, so it's important to work in a place where people can share their successes but also their failures,' says managing director Natasha Guerra. 'It's the people that make the space, not the place. Our philosophy is: you are the companies you keep.'

Created in late summer 2014 by cofounders Alex Hoye and Philipp Stoeckl, Runway East grew from an idea developed in 2009 when there was less support available for founders in the London startup scene. Runway East is now spread across two separate sites between Old Street and Moorgate tube stations, with a strong aviation theme running throughout – a nod to the 'taking off' of startups. It pitches itself as a place of camaraderie: A relaxed, non-exclusive environment all about blending the right mix of people so that each member adds value, be it through a wealth of knowledge and experience or simply enthusiasm.

[Links] Website: **runwayea.st** Facebook: **runwayeastldn** Twitter: **@RunwayEastLDN**

Face of the Space:
Natasha Guerra's background is in tech startups (in fact, she's never worked for a company larger than twenty people), but her family members are all in property, something she's always been interested in. She thought Runway East was the perfect hybrid between the two: 'It's a physical space but also in tech, so a combination between the two worlds I know,' she said.

[Name] # Huckletree

[Address]   Alphabeta Building, 18 Finsbury Square, London EC2A 1AH

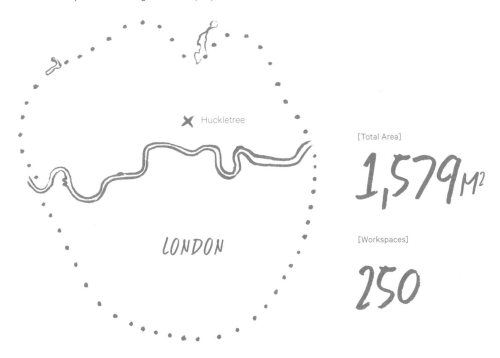

Huckletree

LONDON

[Total Area]

1,579M²

[Workspaces]

250

[The Story]   'Stay curious,' reads a blue neon sign, which hangs proudly on the wall in the Huckletree 'conversation pit' lobby – a motto its founders believe inspires creativity and innovation. Supporting startups, entrepreneurs and freelancers, Huckletree offers a dynamic shared working space that follows a sustainable mantra. Scattered with stretching zones, hydration stations, and indoor and outdoor gardens, it's all about the eco-friendly workspace. Plants that are fed from recycled sink water line the walls, and a monochrome decor is met with block colours, adding elements of fun to a place serious about enjoying work, and growing startups into success stories.

Focused on nurturing technology entrepreneurs, leaders, venture capitals and investors, Huckletree aims to build ecosystems in each of these spaces; a place where young entrepreneurs bursting with ideas can add value to a growing community. Those that want to be part of it can choose from a hot-desking or dedicated space plan to a private office, with pricing ranging from £35 a day to £600 per month. Nestled between the city and the east London tech hub, members can cycle in straight from the street and park in the building's underground bike rack, before grabbing a coffee from the espresso bar and heading to a complimentary yoga or meditation class.

[Links]   Website: **huckletree.com** Facebook: **huckletree** Twitter: **@huckletree** Instagram: **huckletree**

Face of the Space:
Inspired by the coworking scene in NYC while working in the film industry in 2010, Gabriela Hersham brought her idea for Huckletree over the pond after realizing there was a significant lack of coworking spaces in the UK. 'After some research, I brought on board an initial cofounder who managed investor relations, and we raised some money to open up the first space, which we still have today,' she said.

ON CALL

Luke Appleby & James Townsend / Kontor Space

Cofounders

'Bland, sterile, shiny, impersonal – are these the words that spring to mind when you describe your perfect office?' asks Luke Appleby, cofounder of Kontor Space. 'Probably not. We want flexibility, personality, inspiring spaces.' Office space agent Kontor was launched to meet the needs of modern businesses, especially startups, which it says like offices that feel more akin to hotels or coffee shops. 'London is full of big shiny offices fitted out in a cost-effective manner with partition walls and cheap carpet,' says James Townsend, Kontor's other cofounder. 'Generation Y and the millennials are trying to escape that. They want to work somewhere that reflects their brand and [where they] want to go every day.'

Luke and James, both chartered surveyors, started Kontor in 2014 to meet the demand for something different – not least the capacity to change and expand fast. 'We saw a huge generational, cultural shift in what people wanted from their workspaces, and there was no one out there helping startups or established companies achieve that,' says Luke.

In two years, their firm has helped more than 100 companies – 90 percent of them startups – acquire more than ninety thousand square meters of business space, enough for more than 15,000 desks. It works both as an agent for larger firms, helping to buy or lease space for a percentage fee, and finds flexible office space for smaller startups (in which case the office provider pays, so Kontor's service is free).

Flexibility is the most important thing for these businesses. 'People want the same convenience you get in everyday life through tech, whether it's ordering an Uber or getting a delivery with a single payment process,' says Luke. 'Traditionally, companies would take a lease for five to ten years, put down a large deposit and have to fit out the space and look after it all themselves, with all the hassle that goes along with that. But if you're five, ten people and rapidly scaling up, that just doesn't work. That's why you see the huge growth in the coworking, flexible office market.'

3 steps each startup should
take, from idea to scale-up:

- Create a minimum viable product and test, test, test.
- Build a strong team.
- Take advice and choose the right office.

Do & Don't:

Do work with advisors who know the location where you want a space; they can help you avoid legal pitfalls and find the best deals.

Do read the small print! If you take over someone else's lease you might have to 'reinstate' the building to its original state when you leave – a huge cost.

Do focus on flexibility and plan how you might need to use your workspace in the future, and have a break clause or the ability to 'assign' to another firm if you outgrow it.

Don't leave your office search to the last minute.

Don't focus on style above function: a slide in the middle of your office is only a good idea if there's a reason for it!

Don't get disheartened about how expensive the property market might seem – there is always a solution.

The next stage is getting your own space – like a teenager leaving home. 'You've gone off, got your own space, buzz and culture – which is harder to do in a coworking space,' says Luke. But this is also where he believes expert advice can avoid a massive mistake – finding yourself in a dodgy deal at the short end of a lease, with the liability to 'reinstate' the building to its original condition at the end, for instance. Or with huge service charges or excessive rents (which range in London's startup scene from £40 to more than £70 per square foot, per year).

'Real estate is the second biggest cost to a business after people – but often it is largely overlooked,' says James. 'People often focus on the business idea, are very selective about who they employ, but aren't necessarily as thorough and diligent when it comes to the real estate. Why not invest as much time as in hiring people? Creating an amazing workspace enhances productivity and helps attract top talent. Our purpose is to grow with companies as they grow.'

Case Studies

Kontor has helped global flexible office company WeWork find all its buildings across Europe, and assisted similar companies like Runway East and TechSpace – so it can easily match startup clients with various flexible offices. It recently helped Jaguar Land Rover lease a site in the heart of trendy Shoreditch for its InMotion accelerator to help develop its ideas alongside startups.

'What's traditionally seen as a huge, well-established company appreciates the need for continued innovation and wanted exposure to new ideas and technology,' says Luke. 'It's a mini R&D lab for those guys, a 1970s office building that has been completely gutted, ripped back, with raw, original features, concrete columns, exposed surfaces and nice lighting, in the heart of Old Street where the action is going on.'

Shared offices, meanwhile, don't suit businesses that need privacy – so Kontor found young modelling agency Linden Staub a boutique spot suitable for mini-photoshoots, plum in the center of Shoreditch, in London's East End. Even the City is an option for startups, adds James: 'The biggest sector taking office space in the city core, which has traditionally been financial institutions, is now creative industries.'

[Contact]   Email: **ctontact@kontor.space**

[Links]   Website: **kontor.space** Twitter: **@Kontor_Space**

"*Generation Y and the millennials want to be inspired, to work somewhere that reflects their brand and that makes them want to go to work every day.*"

Gemma Guilera & Scott Cain / Future Cities Catapult

SME program lead and chief business officer

Unpredictable traffic flows are one of the main reasons ambulance drivers can fail to reach an emergency scene within eight minutes, according to research by Future Cities Catapult. But thanks to a smart system that works with traffic lights to affect vehicle flow, ambulances in Liverpool – and beyond – could start saving more lives. This is just one project that came into being with the help of Future Cities Catapult, a government initiative to support UK businesses creating services that make global cities better places to live. Thanks to its research identifying the problem, Liverpool-based startup Red Ninja now has the green light to improve the North West Ambulance Service.

'Catapult organizations were created by Innovate UK, the UK government's innovation agency, to reduce the risk of innovation and accelerate the rate at which businesses develop so that we create sustainable growth and jobs,' says Gemma Guilera, SME program lead at Future Cities Catapult. It's her job to connect small- and medium-sized enterprises (SMEs) to problems they can solve, in locations from London's Queen Elizabeth Olympic Park to Belo Horizonte, the sixth-largest city in Brazil. The London-based Future Cities Catapult was launched in 2013, and is currently funded by a £10 m UK government annual grant (with the goal of raising twice as much from other grants, in addition to research and commercial commissions). It is collaborating increasingly with startups that are scaling up and companies that want to go international. 'To date, we've engaged with over 300 small businesses,' says Scott Cain, chief business officer. 'We help startups turn bright innovative ideas into working prototypes that can be tested in real urban settings. Then, once they're proven, we help spread them to cities across the world to improve quality of life, strengthen economies and protect the environment.'

Do & Don't:

Do get critical feedback and learn from it. Really listen to what people say.

Do build the right connections, networks and strategic partnerships. Even if your product is great, if you aren't there, you won't be seen.

Do know the name and surname of the person who writes your check. Companies and clients are sometimes very difficult to navigate.

Don't be afraid of uncertainty and failure. If you can't be comfortable in your uncomfortable zone, maybe you should do something different!

Don't confuse need and demand. Will the client pay money for what you have?

Don't tell a potential client what they are doing wrong! Don't sell to someone – build a sale together.

3 steps each startup should take, from idea to scale-up:

- Build a skilled team you can trust.

- Establish strong strategic relationships, networks and partnerships.

- Really understand your consumer.

Some of these companies – especially those that aren't London-based – might want to buy a £250 'Catapult Carnet,' which gets them ten days of access to the Future Cities Catapult office in the capital. Others take part in weekly meetings and events, and some are sponsored to travel and present their inventions at international conferences.

WhereIsMyTransport, for instance, is creating a data platform to improve public transport systems in developing countries. It won funding to present at Habitat III, a United Nations conference on sustainable urban development in Quito, Ecuador, in October 2016. 'It's simple but fascinating how understanding the real needs of citizens can make such a big difference,' says Gemma. 'Transportation in big cities and in developing countries works very differently. People just put their thumb up and someone stops. So how could you translate a UK system application to those places? At Habitat III, they were able to contact other partners and potential clients.'

Future Cities Catapult also works in projects researching and identifying specific problems that cities face, advertising a challenge for SMEs to address, and selecting finalists to pitch to a judging panel. These are advertised on its website, in its newsletters and via networks including Innovate UK, the Knowledge Transfer Network and the Enterprise Europe Network. A 'Capstone' collaboration with Intel Labs Europe, Imperial College and University College London, for instance, addresses urban challenges in Queen Elizabeth Olympic Park in East London. 'The accessibility of the park wasn't good, people felt unsafe, some don't know where to go so they don't even bother to enter!' says Gemma. 'SMEs with solutions applied to us, and the winners will get £10,000 to develop their projects and demonstrate their solution in the park. They will also participate in events to show their solutions to potential clients.'

Amongst the finalists are one app letting people book open spaces, meet each other and get points for exercising, made by companies OpenPlay and BetterPoints, and another called Living Map which provides user-friendly maps with real-time data to supplement patchy signage. Future Cities Catapult hopes to run about ten such challenges a year, and currently has projects in London, Brazil, Malaysia, India, China and the Persian Gulf. 'Cities are not very good at talking to each other, or even between different departments,' says Gemma. 'We create a neutral space where policy makers, academics, investors, big corporates and small businesses can come together to cocreate the cities of the future.' Scott adds: 'Our work creates opportunities for startups, positioning the UK as a world leader in smart cities – which, as our work across five continents confirms, it really is!'

[Contact]   Email: urbansme@futurecities.catapult.org.uk

[Links]   Website: futurecities.catapult.org.uk LinkedIn: Future Cities Catapult Twitter: @futurecitiescat

"We create a neutral space where policy makers, academics, investors, big corporates and small businesses can come together to cocreate the cities of the future."

Carlos Eduardo Espinal / Seedcamp

Partner

Cash from investor Seedcamp comes with a packed calendar: every week of the year, this early-stage fund has a masterclass, event or trip to help entrepreneurs grow faster. 'We've created a calendar of services, events and masterclasses, an itinerized version of things you can do,' says partner Carlos Eduardo Espinal. 'You can get ongoing board-level support, access to masterclasses, office hours with experts in residence and mentors and trips to the United States, where we introduce people to VCs around the world. There are events in London and Germany to introduce companies to investors, our founders' pack which provides discounts with key tools like Amazon Web Services and a Seedcamp social network. It's not just one dude's advice and money. It's this collective of services, events and a network of incredible people that place Seedcamp in a unique position.'

Seedcamp was started in 2007 by Reshma Sohoni and Saul Klein and funded by a collective of European investors who also wanted to offer startups ongoing support to accelerate their growth in exchange for equity. It now operates as an early-stage funder, offering cash with benefits. 'We invest in founders who have ambitious ideas and want to scale fast,' says Carlos. The fund contributes €75,000 to €200,000 in exchange for equity, and works with startups at two stages: preseed and seed. 'Preseed is anybody who has got a prototype but wants to get to the next stage – build a team, create a company around this and scale it up,' says Carlos. 'In the seed stage, they might have three or four people and are going to market, trying to figure out how to more efficiently target their customer segment. At the seed stage, for example, we have one company that has three deployments with tier one customers [major manufacturing suppliers], but they are all free at the moment. Just getting in the door is hard.'

 3 steps each startup should
take, from idea to scale-up:

- De-risk the team: can you work with your colleagues?

- De-risk the product: does it do what the customer
  expects?

- De-risk the market: are the distribution and price right?

Do & Don't:

Do thorough research to understand your market and customer needs: what will trigger them to buy your solution?

Do develop a prototype, try it and then adjust – don't procrastinate too long in developing the perfect product.

Do invest in your team. For a startup, this is the killer ingredient for success.

Don't worry too much about money – with the right product and team, money will come.

Don't close your options too early. See yourself as a testing lab, rather than fixating on one solution.

Don't lock onto one market or niche. Keep your options open, and don't limit your scope too quickly.

Seedcamp has invested in more than 230 companies since launch, almost three quarters of which are now operating firms and twelve of which have been acquired. At the earliest stage, for instance, it invested in online publishing services firm Reedsy – a firm that does its job so well that Carlos used it himself when he needed to edit and lay out his own book, The Fundraising Field Guide.

'Reedsy is a marketplace for self-published works, trying to take every bit of the book publisher's job and divide it into a marketplace,' he says 'I met the guys – Emmanuel Nataf, Matt Cobb, Ricardo Fayet and Vincent Durand – when they were still in college in April 2014, and just had this idea of how to disrupt the book publishing landscape. They didn't have a product; they just had some screen shots of what it would be like. Over the course of the years, they have built it into an online editor so you can author very quickly, have an illustrator, format it for print and publish to EPUB. I wrote a book last year and I used Reedsy for it. It was great!' Seedcamp also worked with low-fee international money transfer service TransferWise.

'We met them in 2010 when there were two guys [Kristo Käärmann and Taavet Hinrikus],' says Carlos. 'The early days were when banks had so much control of the fees when you moved money around – they thought, can we change that? We helped them scale up and now they are huge, with a valuation of more than £1 billion and more than 650 employees. That's no easy feat.' When Daniel Gandesha, founder of Property Partner, came to Seedcamp in June 2014, his crowdfunding property business – which divides properties into fractional shares for smaller-scale investors – was more advanced, and Seedcamp joined a group of seed investors. 'He wanted to get into investing in property, but realized how clunky it was and built this platform to satisfy his own needs,' says Carlos. 'It's not an easy business – it's regulated, involves sourcing real assets and has been very well received in the investor community as a way of getting into real estate investment.'

Seedcamp has never been an intensive, three-month accelerator program: it wanted to create a place where startups could grow. 'It brought together investors, went all across Europe educating people, bringing in mentors, building Seedsummit.org, making legal documents available freely online,' says Carlos. 'All those efforts were to build the village.' Now the early-stage fund is looking for its next season of successful entrepreneurs.

[Contact]   Email: **info@seedcamp.com**

[Links]   Website: **seedcamp.com** Facebook: **seedcamp** Twitter: **@seedcamp**

"We want to be the closest thing to a founder in that early part of their journey, giving them the money and network to be able to scale their company."

Veb Anand & Alex Clegg / Brand Union

Executive director of strategy and chief executive, Brand Union UK

'There's a famous story about IBM in the eighties where a brown box with the name IBM on it would sell for less than a plain brown box,' says Veb Anand, executive director of strategy at Brand Union. 'The brand was a complete liability. But then they made the effort to think about who they were and what they wanted to achieve and maintain that razor sharp focus to become one of the most successful brands of all time.'

Brand Union believes that startups have the keenest understanding of why their brand identity matters – and is keen to work with tomorrow's massive success stories. The London-led firm, which has twenty-four offices globally, was founded forty years ago, and during its lifetime has given British Gas its iconic flame icon, put Absolut Vodka into its apothecary bottle and designed a modern, touchy-feely message for condom maker Durex.

It defines a 'brand' as a company's defining characteristic, summing up the benefits that it brings to everyone involved. It could be represented in packaging, for example, internal and external communications, logo design or all of these and more.

Today, UK chief executive Alex Clegg says the firm's heavy-hitting clients might include Vodafone and HSBC, but about a fifth of business comes from working with early-stage business. 'Your brand is the reason you exist in the first place, your raison d'être. But – especially if the early days of growth are quick – this can lead to muddy waters very quickly,' he says. 'Look at a company like Uber or Tesla. You can see the strength of that brand, how rapidly it can grow. If you're not ready for that growth or clear about your brand, who it is and what it stands for, then you're going to miss a lot of opportunities.'

Do & Don't:

Do plan for your brand to be the central organizing principle of your business. It shapes the culture of your company and touches all parts of the organization.

Do establish brand governance processes and mechanisms to ensure consistent execution.

Do articulate the values of your brand and make sure they are true and meaningful to your colleagues.

Don't think about who you are today. Think about what you want to be in ten years.

Don't create an overly-complex brand architecture with multiple layers.

Don't skip international legal naming checks and validation.

 ## 3 steps each startup should take, from idea to scale-up:

- Revisit your brand idea every 3–5 years to keep it current.

- Don't make rules people will break: give them tools they can use.

- Engage professional help in developing your brand positioning from the start.

Caring for your corporate DNA is about more than marketing, according to Veb. 'If you don't define your brand, others will define it for you,' he says. 'They will take whatever perceptions they have and that will become how your brand is positioned in the market. Big examples of this are BlackBerry or Nokia, who weren't on the front foot enough to have a true vision for their brands and became more old-fashioned and fragmented until organizations that were once very iconic became a liability.'

Brand Union, which offers a free initial consultation, is a consultancy service that combines strategists, designers, project managers and technology experts to work with its clients, typically for two to six months. It aims to express its client's essence in a way that is compelling, relevant, different and credible by analyzing market context, customer, competition and the company itself. 'We might come up with a narrative, a thirty-second elevator pitch, a brand model – typically, a piece of strategic thinking that becomes the basis for your brand, and explains your positioning in a way everyone in the organization can understand,' says Veb. 'Absolutely like a CV. And it can literally sit on a page.'

Companies tend to call for this kind of service when they are born, merge or are taken over. 'Branding agencies look at brands at birth, marriage and death – with people changing identity or evolving into something different,' says Alex. 'We tend to work with founders and chief executives to be clear about what their business is all about. This goes right through to design work that can be interior design, packaging, innovation around corporate identities, logos and visual identity systems – everything, even from the internal communication tone of voice, language and materials they use.' Naming is perhaps the biggest challenge for startups and mergers alike. 'Most short, pronounceable names you would commonly say or are in the dictionary have already been registered to be used by other companies,' says Veb. 'The challenge is in coming up with something sayable, spellable, that people can remember, is legally protectable and also that works in a multinational world. Something you might think sounds attractive could mean something pejorative in Korean or Hungarian!' Brand Union works to channel your entrepreneurial zeal into a name and idea that should translate into success the world over.

[Contact]   Email: london@brandunion.com

[Links]   Website: brandunion.com Facebook: brandunion Twitter: @brandunion

"If you're not ready for growth or clear about your brand, who it is and what it stands for, then you're going to miss a lot of opportunities."

Gary Parnell &
Maria Luisa Silva
/ SAP

Director recruitment and director GTM for SAP Startup Focus, EMEA

Former employees aren't lost in the jungle once they have left a company, thanks to an 'alumni management' network built on IT firm SAP's software. EnterpriseJungle, a London-based startup, produced a solution that was so good that SAP itself became a customer of the business it had helped nurture.

'EnterpriseJungle is a talent management-focused startup powered by the SAP HANA cloud platform,' says Maria Luisa Silva, head of SAP Startup Focus EMEA. 'Their hero product, SAP Alumni Management by EnterpriseJungle, is helping large enterprises manage Alumni and Retirees to increase talent pools and reduce internal costs. We at SAP are therefore proud to be a customer, using this solution to power our SAP alumni network.' This is one of the success stories of SAP Startup Focus, a program that gives early-stage companies free access to the high-performance data processing platform SAP HANA to build products, while accelerating them on the creation of viable businesses.

'Everybody portrays SAP as a large established corporation,' says Gary Parnell, who recruits fledgling firms for the program. 'When I talk to startups initially, they feel the same way. But SAP at its heart is an innovative, nimble player, true to its startup roots.'

Working with around ten incubators around London, including Level39, SAP reaches out to new companies that might usefully build on its software. 'SAP Startup Focus is a global accelerator where we nurture tech startups focusing on real-time business, predictive analytics, IoT, AR/VR and machine learning, et cetera' says Maria. 'We provide them with the technology, SAP Hana or the HANA Cloud Platform, for them to build their solutions on, and once they have a minimum viable product, we help accelerate their go-to-market and improve their chances of commercial success.' The program is currently working with 4,300 startups globally; about 250 have come on board from London and 10 of these have reached the stage where their solution has been 'validated' to work with SAP HANA. While the typical startup successfully develops a HANA-based solution in eight to twelve weeks, others take a year or more.

3 steps each startup should
take, from idea to scale-up:

- Have an open-minded creative stage.

- Try your product out and get customer feedback.

- Get the first customer, then adjust to the
  needs of growth.

Do & Don't:

Do have clear expectations. It's great to come on to our program and meet potential clients, but you'll need to take some risk.

Do be accountable. The startup needs to do its side of the work for us to do ours. We are both working in the same direction.

Do be unique. The best way to do this is to know the competition in your space.

Don't give up. If you believe in your idea, be resilient and fight for it.

Don't get swallowed up by corporate complexity.

Don't think there are too many hurdles. We are here to help.

'Once they go to market, accelerating a high potential startup can take from twelve to thirty-six months,' says Maria. 'We've picked up companies, like Celonis, that had fewer than ten people when we started working with them, and two and a half years later have over 100 people and have raised almost US$30 m in funds. Then a whole new life begins, and it's about added value, exposure and positioning, and accelerating success.' The program is free, the technology use is free during development and no fees or equity are taken. Some startups may never pay for SAP HANA if it's simply sold directly to the end customer, so their solution works alongside it – and if they do use it themselves, they only pay for a license once they go productive and start generating revenue.

'We definitely don't target startups to somehow enclosure them,' says Maria. 'It's about creating ecosystems of open innovation, SAP opening the technology for young companies to use. In several cases, program startups have been acquired by customers, partners, but also competitors – recently Salesforce paid just over US$100 m for a startup that was part of our program. At the same time, SAP has acquired startups like Multiposting, a French HR software company, and KXEN. today called SAP Predictive Analytics'.

Another example of London startup success is Wittos, which provides 'intelligent' customer engagement via wifi networks and has acquired a number of customers already. 'They are currently working on a rail travel project with the UK government to enhance passenger experience for travellers on trains,' says Maria. 'Free WiFi has been mandated on all UK trains. Wittos is developing a micro-services ecosystem so train companies can provide useful on-board services to offset the cost in providing good connectivity. This might be a service where someone brings you a coffee to your seat or upon arrival at your destination. Or perhaps along your journey a tourism service might suggest things that are nearby as you're looking out the window. It's the next wave of how we will live and manage services tomorrow. It's a very exciting solution.' While working to help the startups in its program grow and make sales, SAP gives them an opportunity to show their wares to potential customers, using its own large network and dozens of sponsored international events. Wittos, for instance, had a chance to be exposed and meet clients via SAP's showcase at the 2016 Smart City Expo in Barcelona.

'The program offers up to US$25,000 worth of credits and certifications during a startup's early life, the developments phase, and the use of HANA,' adds Gary. 'That's just the quantifiable part. All of the mentoring and exposure provided in the GTM phase is worth much more.'

[Contact]   Email: IDA@ida.dk

[Links]   Web: english.ida.dk & universe.ida.dk/startup Facebook: idadanmark Twitter: @IngeniorIDA

"SAP Startup Focus is a global accelerator for tech startups. We provide them with free SAP HANA technology to deploy their solutions and accelerate their go-to market and chances of success."

Svend Littauer
/ Goodwille

Chief operating officer

'If you're going up a ladder, hold tight!' warns Svend Littauer. He isn't telling a personal cautionary tale, but explaining one reason foreign businesses that launch in the UK can run into unexpected difficulties. 'There is a whole how-to-operate-a-ladder guide under the UK's Health and Safety Executive,' he explains. 'Some directors say "this is ridiculous," but they are ultimately responsible for [employee] health and safety, and people like to sue, so I say tick the box.' This is one of the more unusual pieces of advice legal and financial services firm Goodwille has been giving clients – many of them foreign businesses – since 1997. Chief operating officer Svend describes it as a 'one-stop shop' that assists in building business networks and overcoming cultural differences. Goodwille has offices in Warwick and London, serving more than 1,500 clients in the past two decades – helping firms open businesses, comply with legislation and run recruitment, HR, payroll and accounting.

'The company originated from a secretarial role: the company secretary has traditionally been the core of every business, the person who knows the most about an entity,' says Svend. 'That's how we present ourselves, as that centralized controller who can sort out everything for you.' Goodwille was founded by Swedish business expert Annika Goodwille, who completely understood the cultural challenges of doing business in Britain. 'When the English say something, it doesn't always mean what they say,' admits Svend, who has German, Danish and Polish blood and was brought up in South Africa. 'British business culture seems straight-forward, but there are a lot of nuances: if someone says something is interesting, as we know, it means it is actually not that interesting.'

Do & Don't:

Do take specialist advice. Don't just wing it. Things can get difficult and expensive if you get it wrong.

Do research your competition. Use the Department for International Trade and other British government resources. It's a competitive market.

Do network. Tap into anywhere you can to get help – nothing works better than a personal introduction.

Don't make assumptions. What works at home may not work in the UK.

Don't rush. Plan and budget – but if it's new technology, you need to be first to market.

Don't underestimate how important it is to get agreements right, especially employee and supplier contracts.

3 steps each startup should
take, from idea to scale-up:

- Get mentors.

- Be first to market if it's new technology.

- Don't get too attached to your idea
  – you might sell it!

'There's also a lot of red tape – the British introduced administration to the world, and it seems easy, but advisory help is important. Other tricky bits are employment law and finding the right people for the business.' Goodwille offers office space on demand, meeting rooms and a virtual office service, with the cost of its help starting at £1,500 plus VAT to set up a company and comply with business legislation for a year. It can recommend companies within its network for services it doesn't offer in-house (for example recruitment), and encourages clients to negotiate fixed-fee rates.

It typically supports businesses with twenty to fifty employees, including a number of Deloitte Technology Fast 50 firms and more than 800 foreign businesses launching in the UK – for example, Swedish underwear and sports brand Björn Borg. 'We did everything in setting up the business, providing the whole back office support and administration, payroll for employees, handling contracts, disciplinary processes and grievances if anything should go wrong,' says Sven. 'Our diverse client base ranges from "app of the year" winner Readly, a subscription-based app for magazines, right through to frozen cake-maker Almondy.

'Once they grow too big, they often open their own office space, and develop an in-house capability for financial administration. But generally we keep our clients throughout their lives in one way or another.' Although you can start a business in the UK in 24 hours with just £1, Goodwille warns that failing to get the legal work right could cause problems. 'Structurally, they could have articles of association that aren't fit for purpose and are just taken from the standard, off the shelf,' says Svend. 'They might be a subsidiary but haven't taken articles that give control to the parent – so the shareholders don't have any control over their own entity. 'With employment, under English law it's what's written down that applies; apart from a few statutes, the relationship is within the [employee] contract. The pitfall is that you undertake actions whereby people have claims against you for breach of contract or non-performance. And you're not properly registered and not paying the right taxes, the taxman is not happy.' Goodwille also advises clients on office locations and getting the most out of London employees, who typically stay in a job for just three years. 'We are often dealing with high-growth technology companies,' he adds. 'Four young guys came into the office, we gave them a space for six months, they did an IPO and now they are all millionaires. It's super exciting – we see a lot of interesting ideas and extraordinary growth.'

[Contact]   Email: **info@goodwille.com**

[Links]   Website: **goodwille.com** Twitter: **@goodwillegroup** Instagram: **goodwillegroup**

"*British business culture seems straightforward, but there are a lot of nuances and red tape. Get a reputable service provider who will support you and make sure it's done correctly.*"

Gavin Poole & Claire Cockerton / Here East and Plexal

Chief executive, Here East, and chief executive, Plexal

A new technology innovation center in London's Olympic Park wants to link the city's startups together to help them achieve peak performance. Plexal considers its networking function so vital that it chose as its name an adjective that describes everything related to a network of nerves or vessels.

'Our central nervous system controls all the different parts of us, creates our identity out there in the world, enables us to connect to other people, make things and grow,' says Plexal chief executive Claire Cockerton. 'We chose that name not only because it's unique, but because it's rooted in biology and is also used to describe complex technology networks.'

Plexal, due to open in May 2017, is part of Here East. The developer has taken over the last parts of the 560-acre Olympic Park to have their future use determined by the London Legacy Development Corporation. 'Here is a place where many incredible feats were achieved: we won the games, we delivered it on time and the next bit is about the regeneration,' explains Gavin Poole, chief executive of Here East. 'When you walk across Olympic Park and see the scale of redevelopment, it feels vibrant and different.'

Here East – owned by clients of property developer Delancey – has taken over one million m^2 of retail and commercial space, investing £150 m in a refit. Big businesses have already taken more than 60 percent of the space. The hope is that the rest of the space will appeal to startups – with the help of Plexal, a venture created by Entiq (the accelerator specialist behind Level39).

3 steps each startup should take, from idea to scale-up:

- Prototype your product.

- Get it out there quickly to test.

- Refine it.

Do & Don't:

Do fall less in love with your own product than with your customer's problem. Your solution will change because customers are always changing.

Do be bold and don't give up! Here East was criticized for its vision – but look at it now.

Do come to Here East! Join the team, and let Plexal be your innovation partner.

Don't think diversity is only a nice-to-have. Employees with a mixture of generations, genders, disciplines and cultures build better products for the international marketplace.

Don't just chase venture capital money. Look at peer-to-peer, crowdfunding and other financing options.

Don't be put off by Brexit. London won't become a vacuum – it will always thrive.

Claire explains that its unique selling point will be its services, not just its space. 'We are launching a suite of entrepreneurship education we're calling the grit kit,' she says. 'It will really help young companies with some of the practical skills you need early on: sales, employee management, how to manage a social media crisis, how to have a difficult conversation.'

A membership, which costs from £200 to £450 a month per desk, will include access to discounted services. 'We've got a suite of six in-house professional services: legal, accounting, HR, brand, PR and recruitment,' says Claire. 'These provide high-quality, discounted services to the whole community. Our law firm Kemp Middle Little, for example, is providing a free starter package of contracts for any business wanting to set up a supplier contract or sales contract.'

The private firm also intends to start a venture fund, and has already opened a pop-up office to meet demand. 'We're building a founders' community.' Stratford, at the east end of London, used to feel far from the center, but will seem closer when the Crossrail train line opens in 2018. 'This had the potential to be the white elephant,' Gavin says. 'We've proven that with a strong vision and some forethought, you can turn places like this into something quite remarkable.' Claire likes to see it as continuing the Olympic legacy. 'We are the international stage for opportunity and performance,' she says, 'but now it's for the performance of entrepreneurs, technology and business.'

[Contact]   Web: **hereeast.com** / **entiq.com**

[Links]   Web: **hereeast.com** / **entiq.com** Facebook: **HereEastLondon** / **Plexal** Twitter: **@HereEast** / **@plexalcity**

"We want to be an international landing pad for companies from around the world to deliver the economic legacy of the Olympics: creating jobs and driving new innovation."

Department of International Trade

The UK is a global fintech capital

- Investment in UK fintech increased with a year-on-year growth rate of 180 percent between 2009 and 2014.
- In 2015 it attracted c. £524 m in venture capital investment.
- This increased activity makes the UK's fintech sector worth a total of £20 billion in annual revenue.
- Around 61,000 people are employed in the sector (around 5 percent of the total financial services workforce); more people work in UK fintech than in New York fintech, or in the combined fintech workforces of Singapore, Hong Kong and Australia.
- Between 2009 and 2014 almost half of Europe's fintech FDI projects were in London.

London tech startups are big in fintech

Five of London's nine tech startups with over US$100 m of total funding are in the fintech sector, and the city has been growing dozens of startups into global brands, including Funding Circle and WorldRemit. Other key London fintech success stories include MISYS, Markit, MarketInvoice and TransferWise. London has a strong ecosystem to support fintech, with incubators and accelerators created in the capital to nurture and provide fintech startups with access to funding, business opportunities and mentors. These include Level39 (Europe's largest fintech-focused incubator), Visa Collabs, Startupbootcamp, Barclays Accelerator powered by Techstars and Aviva Digital Garage (focused on insurance tech). There are further initiatives fintech businesses in London can take advantage of, including Start Tank from PayPal and the fintech fund from Santander. Innovate Finance is a fintech membership organization launched in 2014. Industry regulator FCA launched Project Innovate in 2014, and established the Innovation Hub, a support unit for innovative businesses to help them understand the regulatory framework and apply for authorization.

London is a great place to do business

London is the world's No. 1 City of Opportunity according to PWC, claiming the top spot as a center for technology readiness, business, finance and culture. It has also been named by Forbes as the world's most influential city. It hosts 40 percent of the EHQs of the world's top companies. Its nearest European rival, Paris, hosts just 8 percent. By contrast, New York is host to just 25 percent of North American regional headquarters of the Top 250 companies. London has a highly supportive government and a competitive regulatory and policy environment, with the lowest corporation tax in the G7. Startups can benefit from measures such as R&D tax credits, Patent Box, SEIS, Entrepreneurs Visa and access to the Digital Marketplace

London attracts the best talent from all over Europe and the world

London is home to 71,000 professional software developers, more than the metropolitan area of San Francisco, New York City or any European city. London has more developers than Stockholm, Berlin and Dublin combined. It has five of the world's top 100 universities, more than any other city in the world, and has two more within fifty miles of the capital (Oxford and Cambridge).

London is Europe's leading center for scaleups

Venture capital investment into Britain's technology sector has reached a record high, with London-based companies securing around 62 percent of the US$3.6 billion raised by UK firms in 2015. With an estimated ecosystem value of US$44 billion, London is the fourth largest tech ecosystem in the world, and the largest in Europe. It is also the world's most diverse ecosystem – 53 percent of employees are foreign, and 18 percent of founders are female. Almost half (17 out of 40) of Europe's billion-dollar 'unicorn' tech companies were founded in the UK. London takes the lion's share of these success stories, producing twelve: ASOS, JustEat, Skrill, Wonga, Zoopla, Farfetch, TransferWise, Shazam, Funding Circle, Markit Group, Ve Interactive and Rightmove.

New in 2017 – The Department for International Trade's Fintech One-Stop-Shop
The Department for International Trade's Financial Services Organization's new fintech
One-Stop-Shop's concierge service will:

- Help overseas companies navigate the process of setting up in the UK;

- Provide introductions to professional and financial service providers who will be on hand
  to assist in the application process, as well as taking companies through the practical
  steps that they need to go through to establish a presence in the UK;

- Facilitate access to market opportunities – the one-stop-shop will work with the UK's
  fintech ecosystem, as well as the fintech, tech hubs and financial centers of excellence
  around the UK, and its network of International Trade Advisers to help companies assess
  market opportunities in the UK and export opportunities overseas;

- Facilitate access and introductions to the right people in the UK and overseas;

- Help facilitate the provision of information about the UK tax system, incentives and
  administrative processes; and

- Provide ongoing government support for companies after they have set up in the
  UK or have sold their goods and services overseas, providing assistance on expansion
  and representing their interests in government.

[About] The UK's Department for International Trade (DIT) has overall responsibility for promoting UK
trade across the world and attracting foreign investment to our economy. We are a specialized
government body with responsibility for negotiating international trade policy, supporting
business, as well as delivering an outward-looking trade diplomacy strategy.

[Contact]   enquiries@trade.gsi.gov.uk

[Links]   gov.uk/dit

"

More overseas financial institutions choose to do business in, and with, the UK than any other country. For an unrivaled concentration of capital and capabilities, choose the UK. "

views

Andrew Crump

Founder and entrepreneur in residence / Mitoo

South London-born Andrew Crump has built three companies from the ground up during his time as a serial entrepreneur, launching his latest, Mitoo, in 2014 as a platform that helps sports leagues use mobile applications to encourage player growth and engagement.

So you're a serial entrepreneur?

Yeah, I'd describe myself as a habitual entrepreneur. Why I say habitual is because I can't imagine a future where I'm not founding something again. When I lift my head up and look around, I see opportunities everywhere, and I find myself driven to do something about them, especially when they are impactful and mean something. I'd also call myself a UX designer-slash-product person; I guess that's where my real sentiment is: product and UX.

So what's the story behind your current role?

I worked in the construction industry in my early twenties where I built a consultancy. I would work for big subcontractors helping them manage cash flow on projects, or as a whole across their companies, but I also built a model that would help them make money out of projects more efficiently. I would bring in other people and help them implement that model on their projects. I then merged that with an electrical contractors company and cofounded a renewable energy company. Three months later, while I had a million pounds' worth of orders, we died when the electrical contractors went bust. So yeah, that was a complete mess.

Wow. How did that lead to what you're doing now?

When the whole mess happened with the electrical contractors I took a year out to relax and figure out what I was doing next. Back when I was a teen I taught myself flash and basic actionscript and I loved bringing things to life, so I decided to get back into what I loved – that was product. That's how I ended up doing Bluefields, which became Mitoo.

Tell us more about Mitoo.

Mitoo is a network for people who play sports, but ultimately its thesis is that in order to aggregate and get everybody who is involved in a form of recreation sports in one place, what fundamentally matters is the data that drives that needs to be brought together. That data is stored in SAAS tools, which are sporadically adopted by sport, country and geography. We first set out to engage sport participants directly, which we were successful at, but realized we could aggregate that data, and that was the key to solving the real problem of the market. It was a significant challenge, but we eventually got it working very well at the beginning of 2015.

So it's going well?

While it has been successful in many ways – we averaged 51 percent per month growth in 2015, peaked at 2.5 million users and along the journey raised US$3.5 million – ultimately, it's about to die or be sold for nothing, so it hasn't achieved its goal.

Why hasn't it achieved its goal?

For many reasons, but mainly we failed to raise the Series A we needed while we were based in Silicon Valley. Mitoo's approach wasn't sexy anymore in mid to late 2015. Entitlement and appetite for risk had changed, and very few funds were investing in anything but SAAS – and wanting to see much higher run rates than they had before, which had a knock-on effect.

Do you think all entrepreneurs have the same characteristics?

For me, I am opportunistic. But I think this is the same for a lot of entrepreneurs; you're frustrated with the way a lot of things are, and you want to change that, and feel arrogant enough to say 'I can impact that.' Maybe that's not smart, but I think for a lot of entrepreneurs, that drive and ambition takes them in directions that aren't necessarily the best for their happiness; we entrepreneurs should probably be a lot more analytical of that process.

What were your early struggles?

From day one, you make a lot of mistakes. They may not seem like struggles at first because you think you're doing the right thing, but you're not. So prioritization, doing the right thing, product, finding cofounders, getting your first revenue or first investment check – if you have not done them before, they are all tough. Getting the first £100,000 was absolutely amazingly hard back then.

"When I lift my head up and look around, I see opportunities everywhere, and I find myself driven to do something about them, especially when they are impactful and mean something. "

Is there anything you would have changed?

I was massively naïve. The thing is that startups are not businesses yet. Starting a business is pretty predictable. Businesses are binary. But startups are massively unpredictable, and I think I came into it somewhat expecting it to be like founding a business. In a startup there's massively different challenges, really different things to focus on, and it's significantly more intense. Ultimately, you're inventing something or taking an existing business model to a market that doesn't have that model, and that presents massive challenges. It also means you'll have to raise a lot of capital, as those things are hard to fund a lot of the time. It's a very different game.

Any advice for people starting out?

For founders: wait before quitting your day job. There's so much you can do in your evenings and weekends, and using that time you can make a lot of progress. In the same respect, a product startup has to start thinking about how to get its product into the hands of users, not just building it – it's the same challenge. You can be working six days a week or one day a week, but you can still make progress, figuring out how to raise the first money or make your first money before you jump into it.

Tell me about the average day in the life of Andrew Crump.

My day's a bit all over the place because for the last six months I've been transitioning away from Mitoo and into other things, so that's really thrown my daily ritual into array. Traditionally, I start early by getting rid of those awkward tasks that aren't actually progress, like helpful emails, which then allows me to relax a bit for the rest of the day. Oh, and I have a wife and two kids, so that impacts things.

How do you make time for everything?

Well, being a founder is pretty flexible, so while you have a lot to do you can still be flexible if needed, and every day you can be home for dinner, eat together and take a bit of time to relax. Then after 8:30 PM, if you need to work, you can.

So would you say you've got a good life-work balance?

I think if everyone worked four hours a day, I'm pretty sure 80 percent or more of things would still get done. There's very little that wouldn't get done. It's true that for every additional hour you add you get more done, but there are just diminishing returns, so for me and many of us founders, you just want to keep working because you know you can make a difference. By the same logic I basically took no holidays, just Christmas, for the past five years.

That's pretty intense

Yeah, that level of intensity – while you certainly get a lot done, it's not sustainable, and I don't think it would be a healthy thing to do again. I think you can get most of that result by being smarter.

Do you feel you give yourself enough time for you?

No, I'm getting better at that now. This year I'm mountain biking, going to beaches and going on a holiday next week for the first time in five years to Madeira. My mum's from there. Beautiful place.

What drives you?

There's a broad answer to that broad question, and I would say it is the same for most people: a need to be remembered, making a difference bigger than oneself, feeling that you're part of something bigger than oneself. Also, the arrogance or ego that says I have the ability to make a difference, that drives me to want to make a difference. And then standard human things like fear of failure. That fear of failure drives a lot of people. It drives me. I try and curb it.

And what's next for you?

I might next take a job for a couple of years while I calm my brain down and not raise venture capital. Maybe I'll start smaller than I did last time, but I'm sure I'll eventually end up back in the world of ego, impact, solve the world, have millions of users – that kind of thing. Personally, apart from going on holiday, I'm going to take a year, maybe two or three, at a slower pace than I've done for the last five, and I haven't worked out exactly what that means yet. And have a side project too. We'll see.

[About]   Mitoo was launched in 2014 and is an invite-only platform for sports leagues and clubs, helping adults looking to play sports find a place to do so, as well as connecting already-active players with their teammates. Mitoo attracted over 1.6 million soccer-focused folk in the first twelve months after launch in the UK.

[Links]   Website: **andycrump.com** Twitter: **@Mitoo_Sports**

What are you reading?
The Happiness Prosthesis by Jonathan Haidt.

What are you listening to?
Portuguese audio books and the Spotify
Discover Weekly playlist.

What's your favorite app?
Kindle, Wunderlist, Tile.

What's your favorite podcast?
I enjoy Tim Ferriss podcasts.

What are your work essentials?
A plain sheeted medium-sized notepad, a sharpie,
a Mitsubishi fine point pen, a super high quality
mechanical pencil and a MacBook.

What skill do you wish you had?
To understand people – I tend to think differently
from how many people think.

Oli Barrett

Cofounder / Startup Britain

Oli Barret is cofounder of Startup Britain, Tenner and award-winning social innovation agency Cospa. He's passionate about making valuable connections between people and ideas.

How did your first business idea come about?

Went to Edinburgh uni for one term, dropped out, joined a kids TV company and became a red coat [an organizer and entertainer at a holiday camp], which gave me a love of events.

So that was it for education then?

Well, I then went off to Leeds University. I had a brilliant time, but I was producing radio and musicals, which gave me a big love of 'starting things,' and that's where I and my first business partner had an idea for an alternative careers company. Ninety-nine percent of companies aren't large, but close to 100 percent of companies that appear in graduate career fairs are large, so I wanted to do something a bit different, run by students for students, that would also give them a chance to meet one another to start things.

How long did it take to become a success?

We grew it very quickly; it was in nine cities, employing 150 people – and the truth is we didn't know really how the business model would work, and although in the end it all looked very successful, it wasn't financially.

So your first business failed?

Yes, but we had managed to bring on board some sponsors including Saatchi and Saatchi, and one of my speakers was Simon Woodroffe, who started the sushi chain YO! Sushi. He introduced me to my next business partner, who was a brilliant guy called Ben Way, who it so happens was the first Secret Millionaire. We just got on incredibly well and he was very technically savvy in a way that I wasn't, and it was just a great combination that helped cook up ideas, whether to launch our own or to help other people launch companies and in return take some shares.

What were some of the ideas?

Well one of the ideas we launched together was a sock subscription company, which was originally called Socks by Box. I was bored in a conference. I wrote the idea on a piece of paper. So we launched that, but another business that we helped someone else to start was called Friends Abroad, which was a language exchange – like pen pals online – and it grew to 100 million members. That was a brilliant vehicle for me.

How did you get involved in education?

About ten or so years ago people would ask me to go give talks in schools, and I suddenly thought to myself: 'Actually, I've had a different idea for inspiring the next generation, which isn't giving a talk.' The idea was more about practical challenges, and that's when I came up with Tenner.

Tell us about Tenner.

Tenner is about giving young people a ten pound note. They have a month to see what they can turn it into. Now, almost 200,000 people take part, it's still going and is now run by the national charity Young Enterprise, and it has spawned a junior version called Fiver, for primary schools, and 50,000 kids did that this year.

What did you learn during this process?

The experiences gave me a passion for starting things that also made a difference in addition to making money, and gave me a real spark to add a more social side to what I was doing.

How did Cospa come to fruition?

I had a two year stint on a Number Ten commission called Council on Social Action, which was chaired by Gordon Brown, and that got me thinking about how you can solve problems by making useful connections between very different organizations – for example, if you want to think about health, you can talk to the government and the food companies and the charities and the entrepreneurs and weave them all together. That thought really gave birth to Cospa, which we called a social innovation agency.

What was the goal of that?

It was about bringing ideas to life with the support of big brands.

My love in life is bringing people together and helping them start things and then putting them into safe hands so they can carry on.

What was your favorite project at Cospa?

The best example was when we helped young people fix their own youth clubs with Wicks, the DIY chain. It's been in over 100 locations with thousands of young people involved. Wicks provided materials, and their customers volunteered to mentor young people, and the club gets fixed and the young people get experience. It's actually really good for the tradespeople's business as well. That's been one of my favorite projects, as it combined lots of different ingredients and it's good for business and the local area.

Tell us about your current venture, Startup Britain.

I suggested to eight people that we go see Lord Young, who at the time was the Prime Minister's Enterprise Adviser, and that coffee, with eight of us, turned into Startup Britain. Those eight people in that meeting became accidental cofounders of Startup Britain, because Lord Young suggested that we be joined at the next meeting by someone from Downing Street, who suggested the next meeting be in Downing Street, and four weeks later we officially launched.

It's always people who you know then?

Yeah, when people hear the phrase 'it's who you know,' they assume it's someone you already know, and I'm always reminded that people are usually open to meeting new people. That's why you've got to push yourself to keep trying when people don't reply to you.

What's your number one love in life?

Making useful connections. This is why I like chairing events. One day you might be interviewing the chief exec of a bank and a startup CEO, and that to me is fascinating because increasingly there's this mutual attraction between them, they are interested in each other and often solving the same problem from a different angle, and that to me is brilliant. My love in life is bringing people together and helping them start things and then putting them into safe hands so they can carry on.

Would you call yourself an entrepreneur?

I think an entrepreneur is what other people call you, but I would never have called myself that. I certainly realized even at college that I loved helping start things, and initially that was radio shows and musical productions, but the idea of bringing all the ingredients together, from the money to the people and the marketing, hugely appealed to me and meant that I could do what I love most, and then eventually work with much better organized people to make something happen.

What advice would you give people in the early stages of starting up?

Firstly, whatever you do, seek out someone who's done something similar before and ask if you can come and see them to ask for their advice. Without a doubt that has to be on the list.

You have a family – how do you juggle this with your work life?

I have some pretty strict rules around spending Friday and Saturday evenings with my family and friends, and I try not to go out more than three nights a week. Increasingly, I simply refuse to do anything I don't enjoy, or work with anyone I don't like. And that means very little that I now do feels like work. And I would encourage anyone else to do the same because life's too short.

What do you like about working in London?

Oh gosh, how to avoid all the cliches. Well, it is an international melting pot, many people will say that, and it's also home to such a rich mixture of industries, from fashion to film to fintech. And there are so many 'Londons' and every visitor will discover a different version, so there's always so much to discover. I love its energy and I love the fact it's a destination for so many millions of people who choose to make it home or visit for a holiday.

What startups should we keep an eye out for?

Loads. I think the way that Tails.com is personalizing pet food is very thoughtful and interesting. The way SeenIt is helping people tell stories using video is very interesting, and I'm excited by the extraordinary growth of companies like ONFIDO, which is helping people do background checks and showing extraordinary growth. And I'm interested in the potential of social enterprises like the Bike Project, which fixes bikes and gives them to refugees.

[About]   Startup Britain **is a campaign by entrepreneurs, for entrepreneurs. It offers inspiration, resources and guidance to help people start and grow their own business.**

What are you reading?
I always read *The Week* and *The Economist*.

What are you listening to?
A selection of terrible 80s music.

What's your favorite app?
Citymapper is hugely helpful.

What are your work essentials?
My Samsung phone and a copy of The Times.

What skill do you wish you had?
Spanish fluency, to play the guitar, to fly a helicopter and to learn mediation and conflict resolution.

What time do you wake up in the morning?
It totally depends. My Jawbone tells me this morning it was 5:31 AM.

Sarah Luxord

Director / Nexec Leaders

It was 2011 when Croydon born-and-bred headhunter Sarah Luxford made her first jump into what she calls 'community movements,' fuelled by dismay with the London riots that took place the same year. Joining forces with two friends in an attempt to tackle the unrest across the borough, the threesome set out to claw back the Croydon they knew and loved and kicked off a series of community meetups.

What were you expecting to gain from these meetups?
We hoped our efforts would bring together individuals from the community to work together and increase business opportunities to help kickstart the economic regeneration of the borough.

And what you saw in return was much more, right?
Yes! Our first meeting of about eight people five years ago has grown to a community of over 5,000 as part of a startup tech scene under the Croydon Tech City brand. There are over 1,500 digital companies as a whole, and it is officially London's fastest growing tech cluster.

So Croydon Tech City exploded. Why?
It's taken off not only as an organization but also a reference to the extremely vibrant tech sector that's now in the borough, so we have essentially been able to support, nurture, champion and connect startups and large corporates in Croydon and support international investment. It's grown into a vibrant community – but it's not just the tech, it's now affected future generations. Our Future Tech City program, for example, offers mentoring, apprentice-ships and work experience to give young people the skills needed to be future tech innovators. We're helping connect schools with other external tech communities, supporting and developing digital learning as well as helping bring awareness that tech isn't scary – for teachers, but more importantly for parents.

Tell us some of the things you've been working on.

We have a mash of events; we hold about two or three a year as part of a learning piece with students, headmasters, headmistresses, heads of ICTs and parents. We get them into this massive event space and separate them out so they can learn from individuals, including tech founders. The kids get the opportunity to do a bit of coding and then come back and demonstrate what they've learned in the last couple of hours; typically it involves building a game of some sort, and the teachers are there going, 'How did you do that?!' From inspirational events to socials to free adult education, our growing community of native and new talent has the opportunity to see each other and interact.

And what's been your favorite project?

Our Future Tech City program has certainly been a work of love. However, I'm superbly proud of the TMRW project. We had the opportunity to work with Croydon Council and the GLA on a £2 m project to bring a new technology hub to Croydon. We went through a vendor process and chose the founder of TMRW, whose vision to create a hub with a twist matched Croydon's growing tech scene. From cutting edge facilities, complimentary services, unique business classes and a community approach, the space is one of what we hope will now be many to land in Croydon – providing one of the UK's best alternative clusters for tech entrepreneurs and startups. The ability to empower others, I think, is the most gratifying piece out of it all.

Did you have experience in this kind of field before?

I had zero experience – I was genuinely just cheesed off by what had happened in the community, and I knew from clients I'd worked with in the past that it's all about the person, the talent and the individual who's leading that. I knew that if we were able to bring some of these people together, and create a movement, magical things could start happening.

What struggles have you encountered?

There've been many struggles, especially in continuity. It's hard to lead volunteer-based work, so the first thing I'd recommend to anyone looking to do something similar is get crystal clear on the vision and purpose and then find everyone's individual passion – you know, the big 'why': why they are doing something, and why they want to do something. That's at the heart of everything we do, it's what motivates us. Be clear on what is needed and by when, understand what the measures of success are – and then, most importantly, understand how you will reward your team. A simple 'well done' or public recognition. It's important to understand people's passions and link that to a clear mission and make sure everyone knows the job at hand, making sure there's continuity, regular communication and it's all aligned to one key mission.

You hear all those stories about companies being built in zero time, but in fact they take a tremendously long time to build. And the key is that it is a journey and a learning exercise.

What do you know now that you didn't before?

That ignorance has its positives. We never thought that the movement would build as quickly as it did, and we've had to be very scrappy in terms of our infrastructure. Also, being able to get the right support on board as quickly as possible, and planning for scale. The scale came without asking for it. It was very organic but very unpredictable, so we were learning how to wing it very quickly, but also tapping into other communities, of which there are so many across London. And, finally, being able to ask for help. I genuinely believe that at the base of things people want to help others, but it's just being clear with that messaging.

What should startups know before starting up?

Trust your gut. The best things that have happened to me, I knew they were good because my whole body lit up. I know it's really cliché, but I absolutely believe in vibrancy and waves, and that's something that, at the beginning of Croydon Tech City, I felt it and I knew I had to do it. I knew whatever was going to happen, I would make it work. Sometimes you can overthink things.

What's your daily routine?

The gym in the morning sets me up for the day. I get up early, head to the gym for an hour and get to work. Because I wear so many different hats, my day can be varied. I try to get some time at lunch time, even if it's just to get some fresh air and walk around. A guilty secret of mine: I might put a Michael Macintyre episode on YouTube if I'm having a crappy day to have a few giggles to recognize there's more to life when you're deep down in paperwork. In the evening when I go home I write a list of the three things I'm grateful for that day.

How do you make time for yourself?

I make sure I'm scheduling time in my planner with friends and family. That might sound like a military process, but if you don't schedule it in, it won't happen. It's important to recognize the precious moments in life, and that comes down to family and friends and enjoying what you do.

What makes you do what you do?

Helping others. From when I was a kid when I used to receive my teacher cards, all of them would say: 'She's looking out for everyone else and not taking care of herself.' I feel I've reached a stage in my life where I have empowered myself, but I feel it's our duty to help empower others, we need to send that elevator back down.

Why London?

Diversity. And the architecture. You don't notice it when you're working in London all the time, but when you have a weekend and finally get a chance to look around and appreciate what's there, you realize it's got some fantastic architecture. I also feel there's a can-do attitude here in London, particularly in the tech scene – it's one of the most vibrant in the world. There's a real hub of community and advocacy for the technology industry here, as seen with Tech London Advocates, which only leads to further introductions and further opportunities.

What London startups are you excited about?

I'm really excited by GrubClub, lead by a lady called Olivia Sibony. They essentially take over unwanted space and turn it into kitchens. They have brunches or dinners, and try to combine offline and online together to create a space for individuals to come together over fantastic food. I think it's an interesting concept in terms of bringing communities and online services together.

So, what next?

Becoming prime minister! Anything's possible! My mission is to be able to support more women getting into senior leadership positions in the tech industry. It's currently only about 9 percent of execs in the industry, and I'd like to see that get to 50 percent – why not?! And I'll facilitate that through my day job as a headhunter, making sure they're getting those positions, but also with the government and by helping to develop our advocates for our working group. And by providing better practice actions for the industry as a whole so we can help empower them for the best actions to take.

[About]   **As well as director of headhunting firm** Nexec Leaders**, Sarah is also a cofounder of the** Women in Tech **working group for Tech London Advocates, where she supports and develops the Tech community, forming alliances with some of the most powerful women in the market and driving forward the need for change and diversity.**

[Links]   Website: **nexec.com** Twitter: **@SarahRecruiter**

What are you reading?
Blackout by Ryan Casey.

What are you listening to?
Fifth Harmony.

What's your favorite app?
Box.

What are your work essentials?
A decent pen.

What skill do you wish you had?
Super flying powers, to get to places more quickly.

What time do you wake up in the morning?
5 AM.

Saul Klein

Partner / LocalGlobe

Saul Klein knows his stuff when it comes to starting up a business. During his twenty-plus years of experience in the startup world, he's been a partner at Index Ventures, where he invested in early-stage internet companies including AlertMe, GlassesDirect and Songkick. He's no stranger to the larger corporates, either: before becoming a venture capitalist, Klein was part of the original executive team at Skype, and was the founder and CEO of what is now LoveFilm International.

You've done a lot. You must have been in the startup business a long time.

Yeah, I first got involved in the internet and startup world twenty-three years ago. During that time I helped put The Telegraph online, founded LoveFilm, was part of the exec team at Skype, started an organization called Seedcamp, which has funded over 200 startups across Europe, and I was a partner for eight years at Index Ventures, an early- and growth-stage VC fund in London, San Francisco and Geneva. I also started a company called Kano, a build-your-own computer business for kids. And now I'm here.

Would you say entrepreneurism is in your blood?

I was very lucky with the role model I had at home. My dad was an entrepreneur, and he started his own company at twenty-three. A lot of my family, on my mum's side and my dad's side, were entrepreneurs, so when I was keen to start a business or join a startup, it wasn't something that was strange or foreign, and my parents didn't discourage me.

So did your parents encourage you to follow in their footsteps?

No, but they didn't discourage me either. I've been coinvesting with my dad in startups since the late '90s, and LocalGlobe is a partnership with him, along with another partner, Ophelia. We're a team of nine now, so I still have the chance to work with him.

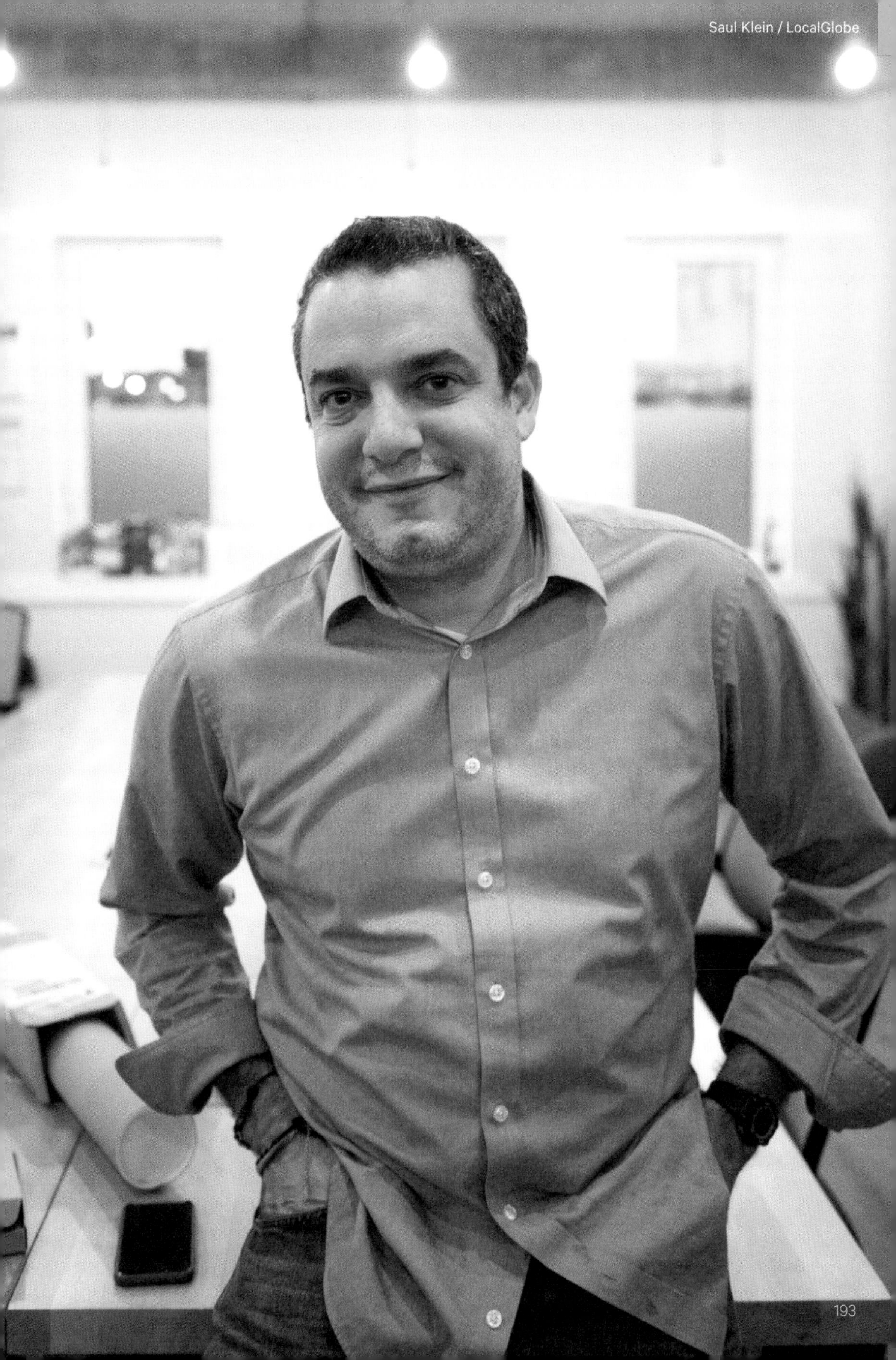

Was any of it a struggle?

I think there are struggles in every one of those businesses, every week, every day and every year, but I think the hallmark of being an entrepreneur is that you try and see most problems as opportunities.

What did you learn from these problems?

There are some problems that are extremely challenging and may take weeks or months or years to sort out, and sometimes you never sort them out. Sometimes you go out of business, and that's happened to me as well, but you learn from all of those experiences and take them for what they are as learning experiences, not a vote whether you're competent or not – otherwise you'd never get out of bed in the morning.

What's the best professional decision you ever made?

I think pitching the idea of fantasy football in '93 to my boss at *The Telegraph* and saying I thought it would be a really good thing to put in the newspaper. At the time, *Telegraph* launching fantasy football was a big deal, but it was successful, and was imitated by all other newspaper groups.

Is that something you learned from?

Well, it taught me that anyone in an organization can have ideas, and as a twenty-two-year-old it taught me that even inside a big traditional company, if you have the right leadership and a great boss, they bat for you and you can do cool and interesting things. That's a lesson that stuck with me for the rest of my professional life.

So would you say you're an ideas man?

Well, everyone has ideas, but not everyone has the confidence to share them. I was lucky to be brought up in a household where it was okay to share ideas, and was fortunate to go to schools and universities where by-and-large it was encouraged to share ideas. I don't think any idea you have is successful until you find other people who you can work with on it.

" *I think the hallmark of being an entrepreneur is that you try and see most problems as opportunities.* "

So it's the process you enjoy?

I definitely enjoy helping to get things started, getting the right people to work with to get things off the ground, but ideas are pretty cheap. What really matters is finding people and turning the idea into something real and sustainable.

What do you wish you knew then that you know now?

The most counter-intuitive things that I still learn on a daily basis are: one, how powerful the word 'no' is, and two, how important focus is. It's just becoming harder and harder for people to stay focused because of the opportunities of the internet, information economy, cities, low-cost air travel, you name it – so figuring out what you want to do and staying focused is a big challenge.

So how do you stay focused?

At times I trip myself up when I try to take on too much. A friend of mine would say: 'Keep the main thing the main thing.' We say yes to too much stuff with the best will in the world, but actually saying no more often and being more focused is often a good recipe for personal and professional success.

What about maintaining a life-work balance?

I try to be at home and with my family at least one day out of seven and then make sure I have my mornings and my evenings to myself – within reason – to provide some kind of structure, because if you're not careful – like me in my twenties – it becomes impossible to not be working twenty four-seven and burn yourself out, like I definitely did.

What advice would you give to someone looking to build a startup?

Aim as high as you possibly can and kick the biggest problem you can find, one that's not just economically interesting and viable but something that can make a difference and impact the society you live in.

What drives you?

I'm just really interested in ideas and the things that people do and what you can make; you always meet people with new ideas to solve problems, or people who are making great music or great art. There's so many interesting people around, so being able to facilitate or be a part of how people are creative, not only in business, is exciting.

What do you like about London?

Apart from the weather, it's one of the world's greatest cities. It's got over ten million consumers, and is one of the largest English-speaking cities in the world. It's got parks, culture, an enormously diverse population from both within the UK and Europe, Africa, everywhere. It's the third best city in the world in terms of billion dollar companies. It's also got more access to early stage venture capital than any other city after San Francisco, New York and Boston. It's also got a huge talent pool of people that work in digital and tech. So yeah, other than the weather, it's pretty good.

What startups in the city are you excited about?

The ones we've invested in over the last five years that are getting to be quite visible or successful are TransferWise, Zoopla and Citymapper, and Index Ventures was involved in Deliveroo, FundingCircle and Farfetch.

What about any up and coming startups?

I think there's a really interesting new generation coming through, like Improbable, which I think is really exciting, Roli – music hardware, Sofar Sounds, which does concerts in people's living rooms, and I'm really excited by Kano..

Any plans for the near future?

Well, to keep doing what we're doing. We created LocalGlobe because the UK and the London tech scene is growing. Although a lot's been done the last twenty-odd years, we think the next twenty years are going to be way more exciting, so we are doubling down on the opportunity we see here. We are going to keep on investing in great companies like the ones I mentioned, and hopefully London will still be an attractive place for founders that want to build big things.

[About]   LocalGlobe is an early stage global capital fund which invests in seed stage companies in London and the UK primarily.

What are you reading?
The Circle, a terrible book by Dave Eggers.

What are you listening to?
Recently I got really into John Newman.

What's your favorite app?
I use Whatsapp, Uber and Citymapper
the most, and Trello for work.

What are your work essentials?
My phone and my Moleskine.

What skill do you wish you had?
Knowing how to code, to draw really well
or to play music – none of which I do.

What time do you wake up each morning?
Between 6 AM and 7 AM, depending
on if I wake myself or get woken up.

Ezequiel Vidra

Chief innovation officer / Antidote

Eze Vidra – pronounced 'eazy' – had a connection with computers and tech from a young age, which lead him to set up Google Campus in London; found TechBikers; start Room to Read, a non-profit collaboration within the London tech startup community to support child literacy charity; and eventually join Antidote, a digital health company that helps to accelerate breakthroughs of new medical treatments.

Tell me about yourself.

I was born in Argentina and moved to Israel when I was 8 years old. I studied business in undergrad with a concentration in IT and entrepreneurship before moving to New York, then San Francisco and then finally London in 2008 to do my MBA at London Business School with a concentration in venture capital. So basically, I'm Argentinian Israeli, married to an American, living in London.

Have you always had an appetite for tech?

I started coding when I was six or maybe seven years old thanks to my love of computer games. I had a Commodore 64 and an Atari, so I had an affiliation with computers and tech from a very young age. In the beginning I started with Logo, and then Basic and then Visual Basic software, as my parents sent me to coding classes after school. In high school I concentrated on computer science and biology. Because I grew up in Israel, I had to do mandatory military service, which gave me time to think about what I wanted to do when I grew up.

What was your first tech job?

In 1999, I was the first employee of Transtitles, a digital subtitles startup in Israel. I had to learn the job by reading the software manual … But my proper first tech job was when I joined shopping.com in 2002, back when it was called dealtime.com. I ran a team there called Dynamic Navigation. It was in the early days of e-commerce, everything was being defined back then. We were doing some cool stuff around structuring data and putting unstructured categories into taxonomies to help users search for the products they were really interested in. I realized then that's what I wanted to do, and everything from then on has had a '.com' after it.

What was your first startup?

When I was in college in 2003, I cofounded a startup that developed text input solutions for PDAs. Essentially it was a keyboard that helped people understand what they were trying to type. It only worked on Palm Pilot, one of the first handheld devices, and there were no 'app stores,' so scaling was hard. But this is how I got exposed to these early stage tech companies, and this inspired me to always want to learn more. A lot of opportunities also came out of my own curiosity, or wanting to play with things and get a feel for how they work. For example, in 2005 when blogging was just starting to be a thing, I started a blog called VC Cafe to learn what the fuss was about. I started writing about startups and venture capital and got hooked on seeing visitors read it from all over the world. It eventually became one of the top blogs on Startups and Venture Capital for a while.

How did Google Campus come about?

I was fortunate enough to work for Google when Eric Schmidt gave a speech that Google will create an 'Innovation Center' in London. I spotted it on an internal site and immediately emailed Obi Felten, then head of consumer marketing in EMEA, to ask how I could help. She mentioned that in a few months they would be looking for a head. At that point, I set up about 30 meetings with friends who were entrepreneurs, investors and accelerators and wrote my 100 day plan. So when the time came for the interviews, Obi hired me to launch and run Campus from when it was a construction site. We launched Campus in March 2012. It was the first collaborative space for startups that Google created anywhere in the world, a seven-story building filled with startups, now with over 70,000 registered members and around 1,000 events a year. Now there are six Campuses, and it's great to see the legacy.

And that was the same year you launched TechBikers?

Yeah, September 2012. We just completed our fifth anniversary and broke our annual funding record at £74,000.

How did that idea come about?

The idea was born after traveling in India with my wife and reading *Leaving Microsoft to Change the World*, a book written by John Wood, the founder of Room to Read. I wanted to do something for kids who are born in poverty. In the early days of Campus, I realized Campus is the perfect platform for that, as I wanted to build community and connections for people that go beyond transactions and partnerships. I wanted to give people something bigger to collaborate on. That said, I'd never organized a long distance cycling ride, or sporting event – I didn't even own a bike. But I decided the best way to start is to just start, so I put a Google form on Twitter asking 'who wants to cycle with me from Paris to London?' In twenty-four hours fifty people signed up, so I was on the hook to make it happen.

" Work-life balance is hard to achieve as we work more and more, but it's about making a place for the important things. "

And how's it been since then?

The first year was hard. We had 27 mm of rain in one day, and we didn't know what to expect from it, but we raised $50,000, and the second year it was more professional and went from fifty to sixty people. Since then the ride has sold out every year, and we've been breaking our own fundraising record, reaching over £305,000, which built over six schools, ten libraries, 300 scholarships for girls, 5,000 books and training programs for teachers in Nepal, India, Cambodia, Bangladesh, Vietnam and Tanzania. We're also expanding internationally – from this year there will be additional rides around the world.

Why did you decide to join Antidote?

It's a combination of things. It was a combination of working on a problem that has real world impact and also a learning curve for me. So I decided to join Antidote after almost six years at Google because I felt like we could make a difference in people's lives and solve a really important problem on a global scale.

Did things turn out how you expected?

When people think about progression, or potentially even success, they imagine a linear line that goes diagonally up and to the right. But the reality is more complicated. The line is not straight, it's round, sometimes up and sometimes down, but as long as you keep aiming to that up-right direction, you're going to be okay. It's important to make choices you are passionate about.

What advice would you give to early stage start ups?

Be endlessly curious. Don't be satisfied with what's already there, always strive to learn more and experiment; push the boundaries. Also, network: tell the world what you're doing, because the next person you meet might change the course of your start up. Finally, it's hard work, so it's about grit. There are times where it gets really tough and you have to embrace the hardship.

What's your daily ritual?

There's a person I wish I was and there's reality. My daily ritual is waking up before 6 AM and tending to my kids. Most of the time I spend with them is in the morning; I try to be present and enjoy those moments.

How do you stay focused?

Coffee is my friend right now. I used to find meditation helpful, too. I did a course called the Art of Living that my grandmother told me to do, which gave me experience practicing real meditation. I felt like it helped me clear the cache of the brain. I don't find enough time to do it now, but being Jewish, I pray in the morning to focus on what's important in life. That's my form of mediation. While I don't sign up for taking religion to an extreme, it helps me concentrate.

How do you achieve work-life balance?

I try to be present when I'm at home and as much as possible put the phone down and go back to work when I put the kids to bed. I also try to get home at a decent time. Work-life balance is hard to achieve as we work more and more, but it's about making a place for the important things. Whether it's spending quality time with my wife, having a beer with friends, cycling or travelling. Not like how Americans have this notion of having 15 days off a year and they don't even take it. I think Europeans are much more balanced. Use the time you have and do the most with it. Work hard, play hard.

What are you driven by?

Impact. Having done Google Campus and Techbikers, I caught the bug and wanted to do something that I really believed in that moves the needle of the world. Or at least for the UK. After leaving Google I turned down a lot of things that were very attractive, to the point where my mum thought I was nuts, but I did it so I could do things that had an impact on the world.

Any plans for the future?

I'm committed to make Antidote a success. If we do our job well, you should see us everywhere. I also hope to scale TechBikers globally, too, and make it self-sufficient.

[About]   Antidote is a London- and New York-based digital health company committed to advancing medical research by transforming the way patients connect to it so that breakthroughs happen faster. Antidote has taken on the massive job of making all publicly available clinical trial information machine-readable and searchable. This means that for the first time, patients can search through thousands of trials in seconds and find the right one.

What are you reading?
I'm reading two books in parallel: *The Gene* by Siddhartha
Mukherjee and *Grit* by Angela Duckworth.

What are you listening to?
Mainly jazz these days, especially Pat Metheny, and Infected
Mushroom or Pink Floyd when I need to concentrate.

What's your favorite app?
Ebay – I realized how easy it is to sell stuff when
moving flats. And Uber.

What's your favorite podcast?
A16Z by Andreessen Horowitz, a venture capital fund.

What are your work essentials?
Mac, earphones, coffee.

What skill do you wish you had?
The ability to absorb information seamlessly and
upload it to the brain. The Matrix, basically.

What time do you wake up each morning?
Sometime before 6 AM – not always by choice.

Russ Shaw

Founder / Tech London Advocates

Founder of Tech London Advocates (TLA) Russ Shaw opens up about leaving the corporate world to be an entrepreneur at the tender age of fifty and kickstarting one of London's fastest growing tech communities, all while being obsessed with 1970s Californian pop rock.

It sounds like you have a lot on your plate. What exactly do you do?

In addition to my responsibilities with TLA and the London tech community, I have been appointed as a London Tech Ambassador by the Mayor's Office, and I sit on a number of advisory boards, including Founders4Schools, Teen Tech and E2Exchange. I was recently appointed as a Scaleup Ambassador to promote the importance of scaleups across the UK.

Wow, anything else?

I'm a non-executive director on two tech boards, one of a public company called Dialog Semi-conductor and one of a venture capital-backed company called Unwire ApS in Copenhagen. I am on the Advisory Board of L1 Technology Fund, an angel investor and a limited partner in the Ariadne Capital ACE Fund, and also the Vitruvian private equity fund.

What's the story in you getting to this point?

For my undergraduate degree I went to Washington University in St. Louis, then for graduate school I was at Harvard Business School. That's part of the reason why I live here; I met my wife, who is from London. We left there and went to San Francisco for a couple of years, and came to London in 1992, and here I am twenty-five years later!

You have your fingers in many tech pies. Have you always been in tech?

Actually, the first part of my career was in financial services, but yes, the second part was in technology and telecoms.

Were they startup tech companies?

Not all. I was CEO of a later-stage startup, but I've touched companies large and small. I've worked for big brands like O2, NTL – who are now Virgin Media – and also Skype. When they were bought by Microsoft that was my third exit. They all got bought, and I thought, 'Well, I've had a good run at this, I'm not going to do this anymore.' But my career wasn't finished.

So was it then you decided to become an entrepreneur?

Yes, when I turned fifty I became an entrepreneur for the very first time, which is when I launched Tech London Advocates.

And why did you set that up?

I set it up because I'd been sitting watching the London tech community start to gain some traction. I'd met with people in the government, including Rohan Silva, who was an adviser to the prime minister at the time, and I met with people like Boris Johnson and people in the Greater London Assembly. I saw what national government and the city government were doing to promote tech, and I kept saying, 'This is great, but where's the private sector group of leaders, the diverse leaders who are going to really drive the tech community here?' I mean from the founder, from the entrepreneur, from the angel investor – all the way through to the big banks, big corporates and everyone that touches the tech ecosystem.

So that's where the idea came from?

Yes, I felt there was a gap in the market in terms of an ecosystem of leaders who were coming together simply to help each other. It was a collective journey from many years of my career getting to this point.

Although you didn't realize it until later in life, do you think you always had that entrepreneur in you?

Interestingly, growing up, my dad was an entrepreneur. He had his own retail furniture business. I had no desire to do that myself; I watched him work incredibly long hours, not have weekends at home...

And you still wanted to do it?

Well, I didn't want to do it for most of my career. But then when my corporate life finished, I thought: 'I still want to do something, and it's nice to be my own boss, so let me try it for myself'. What started as a part time project has kind of taken over my life in terms of this entity called Tech London Advocates.

Was there anything that surprised you?

The surprise factor for me was how quickly this community took off and how many people wanted to become a part of it. When I set this up I thought, 'Well, if we have a few hundred in the group that would be fantastic.' And here I am almost three years later and we have over 4,000 in the group.

"*Knowledge is every-where – and you don't need to go to the fanciest schools or universities to find it. Learn from the people you meet. Stay curious.*"

How many new members join a month?

I am bringing into the group an average of 150, sometimes almost 200 new advocates every month.

How exactly is it growing?

It's literally coming through advocates connecting with each other. The group is open and free to join, but you come in through an advocate introduction. So today, I already brought four new advocates who had been introduced to me that want to be part of the group, so I will follow up with them, welcome them to the group and then they are in the community.

Once they are in, what happens?

They are invited to the events that I do, and are invited to get involved in working groups. Everyone is a volunteer.

Was leaving the corporate world the best decision you ever made?

When I left Skype, the best decision I made was when I said: 'I'm not doing the corporate gig any longer, I'm going to strike out and do my own thing.' Even though it took me the best part of twenty-five years to get to that point, it was the best decision.

So no regrets?

When I left Skype I said I would do my own thing: set up this community, sit on tech boards, do some investing as an angel investor, etc. – a number of people said to me: 'You'll be back in the corporate world in six or twelve months.' But I said no, I don't think I will be. I was getting calls from headhunters all the time, and I said no and kept true to my word about sticking with it, and there was no looking back.

What advice would you give to startups?

I'd say be open-minded, surround yourself with really good people, get outside of your bubble if you can – it's very easy to get sucked into that – and network. It's really hard when you start your own business as there are only so many hours in the day, but those entrepreneurs who build good networks are the ones that are going to be more successful because they know who they can go to if they need help, advice, funding, anything along those lines. I hope in my role I make it easier for entrepreneurs to become part of a ready-built network.

What startups in London are you excited about?

Too many to name! I was at a company yesterday called VE Interactive. They are a tech unicorn, so they are valued at US$1.5 billion, and are in the data tech/retail tech space. They're doing some great things and now have 800 employees around the world. There's also Quill, which is a great content tech company; Technology Will Save Us, they design and build the Micro:bit for BBC Make it Digital; and Unruly Media, who have now been acquired by News International.

Do you ever switch off?

It's hard. As an 'uber connector,' I find it hard to disconnect. I try to turn off by spending the evening in front of the television with my wife, or go places where you're forced to switch off your gadgets like the theater. Or I'll listen to music and zone out for twenty minutes or so. I do struggle to disconnect – it's one of my gaping weaknesses.

What drives you?

Many things. I love helping people and doing good. I like to be recognized for contributions, and I like to make a difference; to prove that something that people think can't work actually can. I like being a disruptor, and I'm not afraid to speak my mind when I think something's not working. I like celebrating success just as much. In my role particularly, if businesses are succeeding, a company is floating, someone's been acquired, etc., I'm on Twitter saying how great it is.

What are your plans for the near future?

I'm looking to build this network further and have created an entity called Global Tech Advocates. So for me it's about driving London tech, and also integrating it into this global tech ecosystem where we can connect with other ecosystems so leaders can seamlessly interface between one group and another. That's the plan, again all from a volunteer point of view. The people that run these organizations are commercially minded, so if there are ways they can make money from this ... if advocates come together for commercial benefit, that's fantastic, but I personally do all of this pro bono – it's part of my tech give-back.

[About] Tech Advocates London is a private sector-led group of 4,000 leaders promoting London's technology sector and addressing issues on the horizon. The group is a not-for-profit community of individuals with aspirations to build and promote London as a world leading digital and technology city.

[Links] Website: soulaima.com Facebook: soulaimagourani Twitter: @SoulaimaGourani

What are you reading?
I'm reading two books: *The Mandibles* by Lionel Shriver and
Connectography by Parag Khanna.

What are you listening to?
I listen to lots of classic 1970s California rock,
I'm a diehard Stevie Nicks fan.

What's your favorite app?
I'm on Twitter too many times a day.

What are your work essentials?
Mac, iPhone and my Oyster card.

What skill do you wish you had?
I would love to speak more foreign languages:
I speak Spanish but would love to speak Mandarin,
German and Japanese.

What time do you wake up each morning?
On average, 6:30 AM.

Tyler Brûlé

Editor-in-chief / Monocle

Canadian journalist, entrepreneur and magazine publisher Tyler Brûlé is editor-in-chief of
Monocle and a columnist for the FT Weekend. The guy that has no apps on his phone tells
us the story behind the success of one of the most respected magazines in London, and
how liking who you work with is one of the key jigsaw pieces in starting up a business.

So *Monocle*'s your baby. How did it come about?

Monocle came about partly because I had an idea for a second magazine for a long time
before *Wallpaper*, so it wasn't just a case of waking up one day and saying 'I want to do this.'

Was journalism something you always wanted to do?

If I go back to probably the '80s, I was always interested in news, not magazines, and probably
thought I would end up working in news or television. But life took a very different course.
I launched *Wallpaper*, and then we launched our design agency. But *Wallpaper* was probably
the magazine I always dreamed of doing. It happened and was successful and of course
continues to exist to this day.

What happened next?

We then launched our branding business, which became an interesting stepping stone to
develop what has become a much broader brand in the case of Monocle. In many ways
it's been a succession of different things, but you can't really look at Monocle in isolation
because it's part of quite an interconnected journey so far.

Had you always set your sights on starting up your own business?

I started my career as a journalist properly in 1989 when I came to the UK, started with
the BBC in Manchester and did a series of jobs in broadcasting, never with a focus on
print necessarily. I was never interested in being a print journalist at all.

So what do you think made you create *Wallpaper*?

It was really circumstance and frustration with the media and working in television and being frustrated with the quality of TV. Even in 1991 I was a bit disheartened by the state of TV news, that's why I thought it would be interesting to get into print, and I think I had a pretty good run from 1991 through to 1995 just freelancing and having the odd contributor's gig at various magazines. Then I went to Afghanistan, got shot and all of the forces that lead up to the launch of *Wallpaper* in 1996.

So you never saw yourself starting your own business?

There was a long track record of doing a variety of things in journalism, but never with the idea that, 'Oh, I wanna run a magazine,' because in many ways I just wanted to be an employee rather than be a publishing entrepreneur. There was no intention of running my own show.

Would you call yourself an entrepreneur?

I wouldn't, but others do. I still just see myself as a journalist, even if I have to fill out an immigration form when I go into a country and it says profession I just put journalist. I never use that overused word 'founder'. I'm a journalist, that's what I do.

What would you say are the main issues in starting up?

I think it's always financing, proof of idea and convincing people to come on board. Obviously the business I'm in is a sales business; you have to convince readers to buy a product and get advertisers to support you and convince the news trade to stock your magazine. So one side of it is just making sure you've got a compelling product people want to purchase or partner with, and to get there it's really about refining your brand and what it's going to be. Also, it's important refining your pitch too, to make sure you can get your foot in the door.

Did you have problems raising cash?

Obviously in starting up any project the main issue is funding, and it took a while. But going way back to *Wallpaper*, that was a different sum of money, we were raising £120,000 in 1995, very different to how we raised £3 m to launch *Monocle*, aside from our own money – and again, a little bit harder, but that was ten years later and we had more experience and more contacts.

" *I believe there's more chance to rest later in life, and now is not the time.* "

So would you say there were any big mistakes you made that you've learned from?

I always look back and think maybe I sold *Wallpaper* too early, but I'm not sure what the alternative was at that time, I don't think there was much of one, I really did have to sell the business. I guess that's informed this time around, but now I have a business which I own over 80 percent of, so it's one that I control with space for other investors .

Why did you need to sell at that time?

Due to cash flow; we'd run out of money, and that was it. Also, we needed partners with some muscle and scale, and it was complicated to launch something which had global ambitions and wanted to establish itself globally very quickly. To sustain that without the muscles of a big publishing partnership was very difficult.

What's the best decision you ever made?

There was no single decision, but I was guided by a couple of principles, and one is: working with and choosing partners that you really like and are in it for the long haul. Both colleagues and investors. Not just people who want to be in and out in three years and get a fast return. Secondly, we've always tried to invest in good environments. For whatever amount of money I've had, we've always tried basing ourselves in quite central locations, and creating anattractive work environment that people want to come to everyday and your clients want to visit.

It's important to run a tight ship, lead from the front to demonstrate in a very clear way so your colleagues know exactly what the expectations are of the brand. You have to be very articulate and focused in terms of reaching people, and the vision has to be 100 percent clear in your head; it's not a movable feast that's ever-evolving.

From your experience, is there any advice you'd give to startups?

I think it's important when employing people that you don't always go for the best CV in the pile, you need to hire a mix of individuals who of course are talented and will deliver the skills you need for your business but are also just good people to be with. The person who is qualified for the job might not always end up being the nicest individual, and no one wants to work with an asshole all day. That's a problem many people fall for.

What does a day in the life of Tyler Brûlé look like?

No day is the same; I travel 275 days a year, there's not a set regime. I would like to say that I get up and run every morning, but the truth is some weeks I run five times, some weeks I don't run at all.

With all that travel, how do you keep a good work-life balance?

I don't! I have a dreadful work-life balance. I think that is often the challenge of being an entrepreneur; if you have a group of people who in some ways depend on you as much as your family does, it's very hard to balance that, so I don't think there's a magic tonic. I believe there's more chance to rest later in life, and now is not the time.

I bet you'll be saying that when you're 75.

Yeah exactly, we'll see.

What motivates you?

Well I love launching things, that's a big part of my drive, so seeing these new projects through to fruition, part of that drive is that once you've built something, you need to maintain it, and it is highly motivating to think you've got 200 people working for you and you need to ensure there'll be enough money for everyone at the end of the month. If that's not motivation, I don't really know what is.

So you say you love launching things, anything on the horizon you can talk about?

We do have some big plans, some big thoughts about new ventures in media – absolutely, such as how do we extend this current brand, how do we take it to the next step and beyond what we're doing at the moment as Monocle. There's a lot of potential in the area, but we're actively thinking about a new media business to launch on top of it; I'm not in a place to say what it's going to be, but it won't be a million miles away from who we are.

[About]   *Monocle* was launched as a magazine briefing on global affairs, business, culture and design in 2007. Today, it is published ten times a year out of an HQ at Midori House in London, and has seen its sales grow every year; it is currently selling more than 81,000 copies per issue, with 18,000 subscribers.

What are you reading?
A biography of Albert Speer by Joachim Fest.

What are you listening to?
A Swedish duo called Norlie & KKV.

What's your favorite app?
I don't have a single app on my phone.

What's your favorite podcast?
As it Happens from CBC Radio in Canada.

What are your work essentials?
A direct non-stop flight, a super
assistant and good luggage.

What skill do you wish you had?
Competence in music.

What time do you wake up each morning?
Depends, but usually 6 AM.

directory

Startups

Boxpark
99 George St
Croydon CR0 1LD
boxpark.co.uk

Courier
Level 1, 88 Hanbury St
London E1 5JL
courierpaper.com

Giraffe360
South Bank
22 Upper Ground
London SE1 9PD
giraffe360.com

Jukedeck
Tech Hub
20 Ropemaker St
London EC2Y 9AR
jukedeck.com

Linden Staub
3rd Floor, 29 Charlotte Road
London EC2A 3PF
lindenstaub.com

The Memo
Wayra, 20 Air St
London W1B 5AN
thememo.com

Propercorn
Unit 1, Royle Studios
41 Wenlock Road
London N1 7SG
propercorn.com

SeenIt
The Smokery
2-6 Greenhill's Rents
London EC1M 6BW
seenit.io

WeFarm
TechHub London
20 Ropemaker St
London EC2Y 9AR
wefarm.org

WiredScore
1 Fore St
London EC2Y 9DT
wiredscore.co.uk

Yoyo Wallet Ltd
2nd floor, Kirkman House
12-14 Whitfield St
London W1T 2RF
yoyowallet.com

Programs

CyLon
Grove House
27 Hammersmith Grove
London W6 0NE
cylonlab.com

Launch22
31A Corsham St
London N1 6DR
launch22.co.uk

**Level39 Technology
Accelerator**
One Canada Square
Canary Wharf
London E14 5AB
level39.co

MassChallenge UK
The Dock, Tobacco Quay
Wapping Lane
London E1W 2SF
masschallenge.org

Startupbootcamp
Rainmaking Loft
International House
1 St Katharine's Way
London E1W 1UN
startupbootcamp.org

Techstars
2 Kingdom St
London W2 6BD
techstars.com

Wayra
20 Air St
London W1B 5DL
wayra.co.uk

Spaces

Central Working
2 Kingdom St
London W2 6BD
centralworking.com

The Collective
14 Bedford Square,
Fitzrovia London WC1B 3JA
thecollective.co.uk

Future Cities Catapult
The Urban Innovation Centre
1 Sekforde St
London EC1R 0BE
futurecities.catapult.org.uk

Here East
Queen Elizabeth
Olympic Park
London E20 3BS
hereeast.com

Huckletree
Alphabeta Building
18 Finsbury Square
London EC2A 1AH
huckletree.com

Interchange Triangle
Chalk Farm Rd
London NW1 8AB
interchange.io

Rainmaking Loft
International House
1 St Katharine's Way
London E1W 1UN
rainmakingloft.com

Runway East
Lower Ground
10 Finsbury Square
London EC2A 1AF
runwayea.st

TechHub
TechHub London
20 Ropemaker St
London EC2Y 9AR
techhub.com

Techspace
32-38 Leman St
London E1 8EW
techspace.co

TMRW
75-77 High St
Croydon CR0 1QQ
tmrw.co

WeWork
115 Mare St
London E8 4RU
wework.com

Experts

Brand Union
Brewhouse Yard, 6
London EC1V 4DG
brandunion.com

**Department of
International Trade**
King Charles St, Whitehall
London SW1A 2AH
gov.uk/dit

Future Cities Catapult
The Urban Innovation Centre
1 Sekforde St,
London EC1R 0BE
futurecities.catapult.org.uk

Goodwille
St James House,
13 Kensington Square
London W8 5HD
goodwille.com

Here East and Plexal
Queen Elizabeth Olympic Park
London E20 3BS
hereeast.com, entiq.com

Kontor
37-42 Charlotte Rd
London EC2A 3PG
kontor.space

SAP
47 King William St
London EC4R
startupfocus.saphana.com

Seedcamp
4-5 Bonhill St
London EC2A 4BX
seedcamp.com

Interviews

Antidote
39 Earlham St
London WC2H 9LT
antidote.me

LocalGlobe
Unit 23 Tileyard Studios
Tileyard Road, London N7 9AH
localglobe.vc

Monocle
monocle.com

Nexec Leaders
4th Floor, 121 Great Portland St
London W1W 6QL
nexec.com

Startup Britain
startupbritain.org

Tech London Advocates
techlondonadvocates.org.uk

Accountants

Adroit Accountax
Unit 8, Dock Offices
Surrey Quays Road
London SE16 2XU
adroitaccountax.com

Arnold Hill & Co., LLP
Craven House
16 Northumberland Ave
London WC2N 5AP
arnoldhill.co.uk

Arram Berlyn Gardner LLP
30 City Road
London EC1Y 2AB
abggroup.co.uk

FLB Accountants LLP
42 Kings Edward Court
Windsor SL4 1TG
flb.co.uk

Metric Accountants
131-151 Great Titchfield St
Fitzrovia, London W1W 5BB
metricaccountants.co.uk

Tally accountants
College House
17 King Edwards Road, Ruislip
London HA4 7AE
tallyaccountants.co.uk

Banks

Barclays
1 Churchill Place
London E14 5HP
barclays.co.uk

HSBC
2 Craven Rd, Paddington
London W2 3PY
hsbc.co.uk

Lloyds Banking group
25 Monument St
London EC3R 8BQ
lloydsbankinggroup.com

Royal Bank of Scotland
Orchard Lisle House,
Talbot Yard
London SE1 1XY
rbs.com

TSB
12 Broadway
London SW1H 0BH
tsb.co.uk

directory

Coffee Shops and Places with Wifi

Ace Hotel
100 Shoreditch High St
London E1 6JQ
acehotel.com/london

Barbour and Parlour
64-66 Redchurch St
Shoreditch, London E2 7DP
barberandparlour.com

Bean & Hop
424-426 Garratt Ln
London SW18 4HN
beanandhop.co.uk

Bread & Butter
7 Enfield Rd
London N1 5EN
@Breadandbuttercafe

The Café at Foyles
107 Charing Cross Rd
London WC2H 0DT
leafi.co.uk/foyles

Nude Espresso
26 Hanbury St
London E1 6QR
nudeespresso.com

Peyton and Byrne
96 Euston Rd
London NW1 6DB
peytonandbyrne.co.uk

Timberyard
7 Upper St Martin's Lane
London WC2H 9DL
tyuk.com

The Towpath Café
36 De Beauvoir Crescent
London N1 5RY
towpathcafe.wordpress.com

Expat Groups and Meetups

London Ladies Club
18 New Canal
Salisbury SP1 2AQ
londonladiesclub.com

Meetup
meetup.com

Professional Women's Network
pwnglobal.net

Soho House
191 Portobello Road
London W11 2ED
sohohouse.com

Flats and Rentals

Gumtree
gumtree.com

OpenRent
openrent.co.uk

Right Move
rightmove.co.uk

SpareRoom
spareroom.co.uk/london

Zoopla
zoopla.co.uk

Important Government Offices

Citizens Advice
3rd Floor North,
200 Aldersgate
London EC1A 4HD
citizensadvice.org.uk

Government service and info
gov.uk

UK Visas and Immigration
2 Marsham St
London SW1P 4DF
gov.uk/government/
organisations/
uk-visas-and-immigration

Incubators in the City

Collider
5th Floor, 22 Upper Ground St
London SE1 9PD
collider.io

Emerge
Block D
Hackney Community College
Falkirk St, London N1 6HQ
emerge.education

FFWD
The Hangout at Unruly
42-46 Princelet St
London E1 5LP
ffwdlondon.com

The Grocery Accelerator
1 Frederick's Pl
London EC2R 8AE
groceryaccelerator.co.uk

Ignite
4 Elder St, London E1 6BT
ignite.io

Pilabs
14 Bedford Square, Fitzrovia
London WC1B 3JA
pilabs.co.uk

Insurance Companies

Aviva
St Helens, 1 Undershaft
London EC3P 3DQ
aviva.co.uk

Chubb
100 Leadenhall St
London EC3A 3BP
chubb.com

ETA Services
68 High St
Weybridge KT13 8AX
eta.co.uk

Lloyd's
1 Lime St
London EC3M 7HA
lloyds.com

Miller Insurance Services LLP
70 Mark Lane
London EC3R 7NQ
miller-insurance.com

Investors in the City

#1SEED
Soho Labs, Floor 5
55 Wardour St
London W1D 6AD
1seed.co.uk

Amadeus Capital Partners
16 St James's St
London SW1A 1ER
amadeuscapital.com

Entrepreneurs fund
108-110 Jermyn St
St. James's, London SW1Y 6HB
entrepreneursfund.com

Episode1
Kingsbourne House 3rd floor
229-231 High Holborn
London WC1V 7DA
episode1.com

Firestartr
23 Berkeley Square
London W1J 6HE
firestartr.co

JamJar Investments
Unit 3D, Phoenix Brewery
13 Bramley Road
London W10 6SP
jamjarinvestments.com

Mosaic Ventures
14 Golden Square
Soho, London W1F
mosaicventures.com

Octopus Investments
33 Holborn
London EC1N 2HT
octopusinvestments.com

Passion Capital
2nd Floor, White Bear Yard
144a Clerkenwell Road
London EC1R 5DF
passioncapital.com

Playfair Capital
8 Warner Yard
London EC1R 5EY
playfaircapital.com

Language Schools in the City

Central School of English
1 Tottenham Court Road
London W1T 1BB
centralschool.co.uk

International House London
16 Stukeley St
London WC2B 5LQ
ihlondon.com

Islington Center for English
97, White Lion St, Islington
London N1 9PF
letslearnenglish.org

The London School of English
15 Holland Park Gardens
London W14 8DZ
londonschool.com

St. George International
79–80 Margaret St
London W1W 8TA
stgeorges.co.uk

St Giles International
154 Southampton Row
London WC1B 5JX
stgiles-international.com

Startup Events

Finnovate
europe2017.finovate.com

London Blockchain Week
blockchainweek.com

London Fintech week
fintechweek.com

Tech Crunch: Disrupt
techcrunch.com/event-info/
disrupt-london-2016

The Tomorrow Fair
tomorrowfair.com

Funding Events

Startup Battlefield
techcrunch.com/
startup-battlefield

glossary

A

Accelerator
An organization or program that offers advice and resources to help small businesses grow

Acqui-hire
Buying out a company based on the skills of its staff rather than its service or product

Angel Investment
Outside funding with shared ownership equity

ARR
Accounting (or average) rate of return: calculation generated from net income of the proposed capital investment

B

B2B
(business-to-business)
The exchange of services, information and/or products from a business to a business

B2C
(business-to-consumer)
The exchange of services, information and/or products from a business to a consumer

BOM
(Bill of Materials)
The list of the parts or components required to build a product

Bootstrap
Self-funded, without outside investment

Bridge Loan
A short-term loan taken out from between two weeks and three years pending arrangement of longer-term financing

Burn Rate
The amount of money a startup spends

Business Angel
An experienced entrepreneur or professional who provides starting or growth capital for promising startups

C

C-level
Chief position

Canvas Business Model
A template for developing new or documenting existing business models

Cap Table
An analysis of the founders' and investors' percentage of ownership, equity dilution and value of equity in each round of investment

CMO
Chief marketing officer

Cold-Calling
The solicitation of potential customers who were not anticipating such an interaction

Convertible Note/Loan
A type of short-term debt often used by seed investors to delay establishing a valuation for the startup until a later round of funding or milestone

Coworking
A shared working environment

CPA
Cost per action

CPC
Cost per click

Cybersecurity
The body of technologies, processes and practices designed to protect networks, computers, programs and data from attack, damage or unauthorized access

D

Dealflow
Term for investors to refer to the rate at which they receive business proposals

Diluting
A reduction in the ownership percentage of a share of stock caused by the issuance of new shares

E

Elevator Pitch
A short summary used to quickly define a product or idea

Exit
A way to transition the ownership of a company to another company

F

Fintech
Financial technology

Flex Desk
Shared desks in a space where coworkers are free to move around and sit wherever they like

I

Incubator
Facility established to nurture young startup firms during their early months or years

IP (Intellectual Property)
Intangible property that is the result of creativity, such as patents, copyrights, etc

IPO
(Initial Public Offering)
The first time a company's stock is offered for sale to the public

L

Later-Stage
More mature startups/companies

Lean
Refers to 'lean startup methodology'; the method proposed by Eric Ries in his book for developing businesses and startups through product development cycles.

Leaning in
A term coined by Facebook COO Sheryl Sandberg regarding gender differences in assertiveness and the resulting discrepancies in recognition, opportunities and pay in the workplace

M

M&A
(Mergers and Acquisitions)
A merger is a combination of two companies to form a new company, while an acquisition is the purchase of one company by another in which no new company is formed

MAU
Monthly active user

MVP
Minimum viable product

P

P2P
A network created when two or more PCs are connected and sharing resources without going through a separate server

Pitch Deck
A short version of a business plan presenting key figures

PR-Kit (Press Kit)
Package of pictures, logos and descriptions of your services

Pro-market
A market economy/a capitalistic economy

R

Runtime
The amount of time a startup has survived

S

SaaS
Software as a service

Scaleup
Company that has already validated its product in a market, and is economically sustainable

Seed Funding
First round, small, early-stage investment from family members, friends, banks or an investor

Seed Investor
An investor focusing on the seed round

Seed Round
The first round of funding

Series A/B/C/D
The name of funding rounds coming after the seed stage

Shares
The amount of the company that belongs to someone

Startup
Companies under three years old, in the growth stage and becoming profitable (if not already)

SVP
Senior Vice President

T

Term Sheet/Letter of Intent
The document between an investor and a startup including the conditions for financing (commonly non-binding)

TCP/IP protocols
Transmission Control Protocol and Internet Protocol

U

UX
(User experience design)
The process of enhancing user satisfaction by improving the usability, accessibility and pleasure provided in the interaction between the user and the product.

Unicorn
A company worth over $1 billion

V

VC (Venture Capital)
Outside venture capital investment from a pool of investors in a venture capital firm in return for equity.

Vesting
Employee rights to employer-provided assets over time, which gives the employee an incentive to perform well and remain with the company

VR
Virtual Reality

About the Guide

Based on the idea of a traditional guidebook to carry with you everywhere, the guides are made to inspire a generation to become more successful entrepreneurs through case-stories, advice and expert knowledge. Useful for when you start a project or business, the guide gives insight on where to go, who to talk to and what not to miss from the local people who know the city best.

How we make the guides:

To ensure an accurate and trustworthy guide every time, we team up with a local city partner, ideally an established organization with experience in the local startup scene, who conducts a general call out to the local community to nominate startups, coworking spaces, founders, incubators and established businesses through an online submission form. These submissions are narrowed down to the top fifty selected companies and individuals. The local advisory board then votes anonymously for the final selection to represent the range of industries and startup stories in the city. The local team, in close collaboration with our editorial and design team in Berlin, then organize and conduct the necessary interviews, photoshoots and research, using local journalists and photographers. All content is then reviewed, edited and approved by the Startup Guide team in Berlin and Copenhagen HQ, who are responsible for the final design, layout and print production.

 Who makes the guides:

Sissel Hansen – Founder / CEO

Thomas Nymark Horsted – Cofounder / COO

Jenna van Uden – Editor

Senay Boztas – Staff Writer

Laurence Currie-Clark – Copyeditor

João Mira – Marketing and Sales Manager

Maurice Redmond – Art Director

Tim Rhodes – Production Manager

Sanjini Redmond – Illustrator

Daniela Carducci – Photo Editor

Anka Cybis – Graphic Designer

 Contact us at info@startupeverywhere.com

#startupeverywhere

Startup Everywhere is a creative content and self-publishing company that produces the **Startup Guide**. We develop, produce and distribute high quality content and tools to help you navigate in the local and global startup scene. Tailored to aspiring entrepreneurs, founders, freelancers, startups, investors and enthusiasts, it is a place to find inspiration, advice, specific local information and access to a growing network.

 Email info@startupeverywhere.com to get in touch with us.

Startup Guide Maps

The perfect navigational companion to the Startup Guide.
Startup Guide Maps is available on **iOS** and **Android**,
the app features all the coworking spaces, incubators,
accelerators and cafés with wifi in the cities that have
a guide.

The Startup Everywhere Community

Join the global community for entrepreneurs, founders,
startups, investors and enthusiasts. Find your local network,
get feedback, and access talent, know-how and much more.

The Startup Guide Bookstore

Order a copy online and begin exploring the local startup
scenes of Berlin, Copenhagen, Aarhus, Stockholm, Oslo,
Lisbon, Trondheim, London and Vienna, with many more
to come. You click, we ship.

 startupeverywhere.com

Follow us: instagram.com/startupeverywhere

With thanks to our content sponsors

plexal

Goodwille.

WHERE NEXT?